Gone the Sun

by
Joel Peckham

UnCollected Press

Gone the Sun
Copyright © 2024 by Joel Peckham

All rights reserved. This book in full or partial form may not be used or reproduced by electronic or mechanical means without permission in writing from the author and UnCollected Press.

Cover Art: Lily Jurskis

Back Cover Portrait: Austin O'Connor

Book Design by: Joel Peckham & Henry Stanton

UnCollected Press
8320 Main Street, 2nd Floor
Ellicott City, MD 21043

For more books by UnCollected Press:
www.therawartreview.com

First Edition 2024
ISBN: 979-8-9883022-9-2

The measure and scope of a person, his powers, lie in his ability to transform the lives of those around him—Amélie O. Rorty, *The Identities of Persons*

Wherever you are, you are here—John Lennon

In Loving Memory of Joel Peckham Sr.,

1940-2022

for Jeanne Peckham

*

"You just don't understand," my father says. The bones of his jaw locked tight, eyes drifting somewhere past the bright green ball fields of Camp Manitou and on into the deeper greens of the forests of central Maine. I try to track his gaze. The morning mist has already burned away. The sun shining wetly on asphalt courts. *It's going to be a hot one*, I think. Hot and wet. Air you need to swim through. And I'm thankful for my little band room in the back of the rec hall with the floor-mounted air conditioner—it has become a safe space for me. For staff members I will find there practicing guitar or drums with headphones on or sometimes just lying on the floor and staring up at the ceiling when they have a spare hour away from the kids. I am almost always there now. The one place where I don't feel lonely or anxious or at least where loneliness and anxiety feel manageable. Something I can arrange and control. My father is angry. Again. It has been a summer of anger. A summer of small spontaneous explosions and storms that would be almost rhythmic if only for their frequency. Almost predictable. But not quite. And to be almost in rhythm, to have almost a pattern is more unnerving than pure randomness. My mother and I have spent the past weeks jarred and shuddered, unsettled and uneasy, always in a state of baffled anticipation. Though some things have become almost comically predictable. Part of our routine. A normal day. Already my father has exploded into a rage at my mother for hiding his tool bag, only to find it where he left it on the floor of his golf cart. Already he has threatened to punch Robert (Waldo) Waldstein in the mouth. Already he has stormed away in the middle of the early morning meeting, grumbling something about "stupid assholes," waving his hands behind him in dismissal. The other directors used to stare at me as he hopped off in his cart and tore away to line a soccer field or reorganize the baseball shed, every face conveying the same question, "What the hell was that about?" But after several weeks, several summers of this, no one really pays it much attention. It's to be expected. Even joked about. His anger used to have a sting to it, his threats real power, but now he is shrugged off like one of the sudden squalls that can come in over the lake. No matter how bad it gets, you know it won't last long or change anything. In a few minutes the wind will stop, the lake will calm, and the sun will come streaming through the clouds. All you have to do is duck inside or stand beneath an awning and wait it out. But for people who are close to him, the cumulative effect can be wearing. Exhausting.

As for me, I can't listen to my father without his rage triggering the memory of a frightened little boy hiding in his room with his hands covering his ears. Or the 12-year-old who'd saved up enough money from his paper route to purchase his first little cassette player, a yellow RCA model designed to look exactly like the Sony Walkman all of my friends had, but at half the price. When my father came home angry, I'd pop a Beatles or Aerosmith CD in and turn the volume up high, drowning the world in Rock and Roll. In some ways, I become that boy, turning inward, tuning out and off.

    A few minutes earlier my mother and I had been eating breakfast along with nearly five hundred boys and staff in the large wood and concrete dining hall whose horrible acoustics take each uttered word and round it, somehow both amplifying and blurring, converting everything into a droning hum accented by the clatter of plates and forks, the occasional dropped tray that ripples first into laughter, then ironic applause. You do not converse here so much as shout and outshout those around you, attempting to be heard above the oceanic murmur of children, a sound that seems to slowly grow in volume before crescendoing in a call for quiet, announcements, and the hectic break for the swinging front doors. I rarely speak at meals, quietly planning my day and eating rubbery eggs and salty turkey-bacon, my head full of pop songs I'm always arranging and rearranging in my head, before getting up and individually checking in on my staff one at a time, making sure no one has had too good or bad a night and slept through breakfast, letting them know what periods I need them for and which one they can skip, sneaking off into the parking lot for a cigarette or stealing a shower in an empty cabin. Sometimes I sit for a second to talk about a song idea for the kids or just put a hand on a shoulder and say good morning. I love my staff like family. And this summer I am more dependent upon them than ever. This is my first summer at camp without my wife or son and I've been lonely, needy, and torn between worlds. Increasingly dependent on ritual and routine to keep from shaking apart.

*

    I know something about rhythm, about time and tempo. When I write, I read my sentences out loud to myself to test their pace. Sometimes I lie in the quiet and listen to my breath and my heartbeat or the pulse of the pump house down by the lake. Rhythm is life. Is peace. I have been teaching music at this summer camp for nearly ten years and it is always the drummer and the bassist I find myself listening to the most, the groove. There is no art without pattern. And much of what makes a band cohere is learning to find the one. The first beat in a measure when it comes around again. Four people. One heartbeat. And the thrill of variation within that pocket where everything is rhythm within rhythms. And though I am shy around people it is their rhythms that I pay the most attention to. Sometimes I think my need to constantly speak may be an effort to drown some of that out, to protect myself from the constant clatter of heartbeats within heartbeats. To try to force everything into sync.

    I was a very quiet child—inward, somber. Prone to be lost in my own world, but also always listening. Always one ear to the track. Even as a young boy I remember sitting on the bleachers as my father would coach, running an almost balletic infield/outfield at the end of practice, a routine perfected over decades of coaching. Every coach starts a game by hitting grounders to his team, but my father had turned the practice into art, his players so well drilled that I am certain he won more than a few games (especially in the summer against ragtag, poorly uniformed summer camp teams) before they even began. It was just so obvious that he knew what he was doing and everyone else was just pretending to.

    Long before I was a writer or a singer, I was a listener. And I remember how I would close my eyes, attentive, first to the chiming ping of the ball coming off his bat, then the voice of the catcher positioning the cutoff man, then my father's occasional grunting commands. "Come on, spot the ball, catch it on the run. Jesus Christ, Feldman, move up on the grass. Don't let the ball play you. Always know what you're going to do before you start to do it. Bases, outs, and you. Who's on base, how many outs, what am I going to do when the ball comes to me. That's it. Good throw. Next time, drop to a knee and shovel it. Like this. Exactly."

    Though my father had a beautiful singing voice and sang baritone in the church choir through my early childhood, years of grunting and shouting at his players (and his family) had roughened it around the edges. But any vocalist can hit the notes. My father had timing, or rather, instinctively understood timing. And every word. Each curse or encouragement seemed placed to greatest effect, part of the overall composition. Both improvised and intentional. He could rattle you, soothe you, build you up and break you down with just a handful of well-placed words. Some players couldn't take it. Pitchers especially had to have a tough skin. He could get into a player's head without being fully conscious he was doing so. One player in particular, blessed with what my father called a million-dollar arm and a ten-cent head, had become so focused on my father's reactions that he would look into the dugout after every pitch, ball or strike, infield grounder or homerun. "Why does he keep doing that," my father would ask everyone around him. And no one had the courage to even venture an answer to a question so obviously rhetorical. But I loved to listen to my father's voice and all its colors, its depth and shape. And I know this doesn't make much sense, but I still think of sound this way, not in terms of volume or pitch but distance and size, location and space. I would try to listen into a thing or past it or try to push through the surface noises, aluminum on leather, the chatter of players, the distant purr of a mower, the shoosh, rattle, and rumble of a logging truck driving too fast down the road bordering the fields—in and out and down. Even the white noise of an oscillating fan or the engine of a ski boat seemed composed of so many notes and colors, so much depth, that I would feel overwhelmed by it. All of this is to say that often when I seem most distracted is when I am paying the closest attention, just not to what everyone else is. And if I care about a person, I know his or her rhythms. I adapt to them. Slowly working my way into the composition they are making without knowing it.

  If I don't care, if I'm not interested, or if I feel that a person may be toxic or simply boring, that person flattens out. It's the difference between noise and music. I can feel myself walling off, shutting them out. I can't and wouldn't wall my father off. I wouldn't know the first thing about how to do it. Though I have certainly tried. I know my father's rhythms and find them maddening and beautiful. As a child I had learned to track his mood, knowing when I could get close to him or when I'd need to approach carefully as if he were something wild. I remember when he'd come home from games he'd lost (and in his mind it was always *his* fault, *his* mistake) and I could feel his simmering frustration, a low boiling rage that could explode at any time. I do not want to suggest that my father was abusive or violent. I can think of only one time when he ever raised a hand to me. But there was, at these times, a violence and buzzing pressure about him that could be felt. And it was often terrifying, sometimes exhilarating.

  This morning had been one of those days when it looked as if my father would either skip or forget about breakfast completely. After he stormed out of yet another morning meeting and zipped off to the fields, my mother and I had walked up to breakfast together, taking it very slowly so as not to aggravate her recently repaired knee, letting the youngest campers weave around us, running full speed up the hill to try to reach the dining hall first because, well, I honestly don't know. Because they are boys and this is camp and everything is a competition. It's a nice walk nonetheless, a winding path uphill, past cabins and beneath the shade of hundred-year-old birch and oak. "He's been in such a bad mood, Jo. Every day. I just wish we could get him to stop going to those meetings. They confuse and frustrate him. And he really doesn't need to be there. And every time it's the same thing. He goes, he feels disrespected. He storms away on his cart, and I'm left hobbling up the hill without him and worrying about whether or not he'll show up for breakfast. Maybe you could talk to him?"

    I nod my head. And I will talk to him. Talking to and keeping track of my father has been one of my unacknowledged jobs at camp for several summers now. But I also know that talking to him about this will do little good. Not because he won't listen (he might) and not because he is stubborn (he is) or even because telling him he doesn't need to be there will make him feel angrier (it will). The problem is, even if I can convince him to skip the meetings, that the meetings are ridiculous, that he has better things to do; even if I get him to promise me, hand to God, that he will never go to another damned morning meeting, after one night of sleep he will have forgotten we had even had that conversation. Reveille will come blaring out of the speaker attached to the roof of his cabin. He'll throw on his gray polyester coaching shorts and ball cap and stand outside the office, arms crossed over his barrel-chest, already frustrated and furious. The first one there, ready to tell anyone who will listen just how stupid these meetings are and how for a good thirty years, the "morning meeting" consisted of himself, the camp owners, and the programming director planning the day over breakfast. "The whole thing was over in about a minute and a half. Now it's everybody and everybody's assistant. We got a million things going on at once and everyone and no one is in charge. I got teenagers telling me what to do and where to go. Too many cooks in the kitchen." He's not wrong. Since my father first arrived as Athletic Director in 1970, the camp has nearly outgrown its capacity, from about 150 boys, 80 staff, and maybe 10 directors, to nearly 400 campers, over 150 counselors and, absurdly, nearly 30 directors in charge of everything from camper-parent relations to music, to wellness, to the culinary arts. Some of the directorships are necessary, the consequence of trying to control and accommodate an ever-growing, increasingly diverse population of young boys. Part of it is just silly, the product of the owners wanting to give people they like and value a role and keep them around for years after they are no longer willing or able to spend their nights sleeping in a cabin full of boys. My position is a case in point. Being director of camp Manitou's music program is a little like being major general of a navy consisting of one rowboat in a desert. The music program didn't even exist when I was made director of it (after some shaky stints as Assistant Athletic Director, Programming Director, Junior Camp Programming Director, and Head of Baseball). I suspect that had I not been a Peckham, I might not have been asked to return.

But I was a Peckham, and in the early 2000s that still meant something. My family legacy is permanently stamped on this place, complete with a to-scale replica of Fenway (Citgo sign and all) dominating the playing fields, PECKHAM PARK painted in three-foot tall white block letters across its own Green Monster (this despite both owners being ardent Yankee fans). Thus, a position was created for me. And my apparent ability to play three open chords on guitar while singing qualified me to create and run a music program. So with a budget of about 250 dollars, I bought some electric guitars and a bass from a pawn shop, salvaged an old Yamaha keyboard, re-assembled a drum-kit from pieces I found underneath a stage and went about establishing my own little school of rock among the pine trees of Oakland, Maine. When you can only play three-chord rock songs and know one scale (minor pentatonic), you teach kids how to play Creedence Clearwater Revival, The Ramones, and Bob Dylan. Finding people willing to listen to the resulting racket is another challenge entirely. Still, ten years of determined effort and relentless advocacy had made my little program part of the fabric of camp life. And if, like me, it is somewhat awkward and ill-fitting, I wouldn't really have it any other way.

Despite having been a two-sport college athlete, a former camper and counselor here with decades of experience, an educator who enjoys working with children, and a former coach, I am not a natural fit for Manitou and never really have been. It's not that I didn't enjoy being a camper here. I loved it, counting down the days after Christmas break, literally crossing out the boxes from January to June. I loved the smell of the place—a heady scent of damp leaves, mud and cut grass, the constant buzzing excitement of it, even at night, its *aliveness*. Unlike my father and sisters, I have never been a natural athlete and struggle in competitive situations, though constant practicing, weight training, persistence and a desire to please my father got me to a point where I was better than average at baseball and football. What I truly loved about camp had almost nothing to do with sports. I could do sports at home. In fact, in my household participating in athletics was not so much an expectation as an assumption—a part of what it meant to be a Peckham. But I was a lonely, introverted kid with relatively few friends, two older sisters whose talents in gymnastics and dance kept them in gyms and studios most of the day, and parents who worked until five or six in the evening. When I wasn't playing a sport, I was alone quite a bit—especially in the winter when the house was quiet and still. It was difficult to feel lonely at Manitou. That may have been a large part of why I returned after the accident. Darius was an only child and our little apartment in New Hampshire could get very quiet. Too quiet.

For years the greatest perk of being the "band director" at this all-boys sports camp was not having to show up for morning meetings. Or the line-up for flag raising, or for anything I didn't feel like doing. Which was pretty much anything not relating to music. At a place where the schedule is everything, I defiantly kept my own. The rickety cabin I shared with the lacrosse director was right next to the dining hall, so I'd roll out of bed and wander into breakfast for coffee and maybe a hardboiled egg, talk to my staff, then wander out, egg and coffee cup in hand, and set up the band room, then sit there as the air conditioner cooled the place down, strumming my guitar and working out harmonies. My friend Corey, the head counselor, used to tease me about it. "Juniah," he'd say in his thick south Boston accent, occasionally throwing a forearm into my shoulder or pulling me into a violent hug, "I see you missed the morning meeting again?"

"You noticed that, huh? Sorry, won't happen again. If it does, you can walkie me. You can always reach me if there's a music-related emergency."

"That would work if you carried a walkie."

"It's in the band-room."

"Uh huh. Shuah." I don't mention that it's never on or even charged and that I would be hard pressed to even find it buried in the toolbox where we keep extra strings, batteries, and wire-cutters. But I suspect he knows this. I half suspect it might have been stolen by one of the campers. He probably knows this too. Not carrying a walkie talkie is another benefit of being relatively invisible. For someone who is hypersensitive to sound, the constant squawk, chatter, buzz, and whistle of those devices is beyond aggravating. I also have a bad habit of losing the damned things or leaving them out in the rain. I realize that Corey could have probably fired me or have me "not asked back" for about fifty different reasons. Corey won't fire me. Because for whatever reason, Corey likes having me around. Likes my program and will, on occasion, stop in during a band rehearsal and grab the microphone. Everyone on staff can play Rage Against the Machine's "Killing in the Name of" just so Corey can step up to the mic and scream along when he gets the urge. Corey's tough guy South Boston hockey player shtick is intimidating only if you don't really know him. The guy is a licensed psychologist with multiple advanced degrees. He might look like a thug in his Boston Bruins t-shirt and Red-Sox hat, and could almost certainly handle himself in a bar fight, but he's too smart to get into a bar fight. "C'mon, Core. You have my number. Call me if you need me." I do carry my phone on me at all times which is, of course, against camp rules (how else will I look up chords and lyrics). Another one of my many little rebellions. Like refusing to ever wear a staff shirt (with the exception of visiting day or performances), drinking and smoking with my staff at night, or canceling instructional periods to take my staff downtown for an equipment run (one staff member for each package of strings) and to get breakfast and coffee at the local cafe. Or skipping meals and morning meetings. A place and its culture might influence who we are, but it is how we interact with it that defines us. I have long since stopped trying to change this world to fit me—except in incremental ways; but I have learned to navigate its gaps and spaces, have come to take joy in them. And I have made room here—*a room*—for myself and for the people I love.

In my first years back at Manitou, well before I launched the music program, while I was still in nearly constant pain and trying to rehabilitate my body and mind, Corey and I would take long, slow jogs together on Route 137, a rolling, two-lane logging highway that runs along both East and North Ponds. Corey would listen as I talked about the accident, about Susie and Cyrus, about Rachael, about how hard I was working to take back control of my life, to get myself together for Darius. "I feel like I'm always on the edge of something, you know? I have nightmares that I'm in this van with everyone I love and then I just realize that one of them is gone, then another, and I want to stop the van and look for them, but I can't. Until I'm alone and I'm just driving by myself." Back then I would have panic attacks any time I didn't know where Darius was. He was so little—just four years old. And I was trying to work. And trying to parent. And trying to get my head straight. Every day was impossible. And every day was a miracle. "Even right now, man, even when I'm awake. I'm running with you and that's great, but a part of me can't shake the feeling that a truck could come over that hill at any moment and just take us both out. Or maybe we get back to camp and something will have happened to Darius."

"That's just being alive, buddy. That's true for everyone every day. Considering what you've been through, I'm surprised your nightmares aren't worse. I'm surprised you can do anything. But here you are. Doing it. You just need to get back in the moment you're in. Trust me. You're doing all the right things. So you're scared. But you're still here, right? You're hurting, but you're still running, right? Just keep doing what you're doing."

Corey understands me as well as anyone I know. Gets me just enough to give me the slack I need to do what I do and maybe a little more than that. He can see the joy in it, but also its necessity in a place like this. My program caters to a different kind of kid (and counselor). Not all of our campers are athletes and even the ones who are, aren't really that good. The various art programs—music, culinary, video, theater—speak to our increasingly nonathletic camper population. But even those programs attract relatively traditional campers. My program caters to a different kind of kid entirely. The loners. The socially awkward. The creative and sensitive. Kids who grow their hair long or dye it strange colors and hide their eyes behind the bangs. Kids who show up in jeans and slippers to the track meet and who sit back on the bleachers during socials with our sister camp, Matoaka. Kids who DON'T race each other up the hill. Kids who don't participate in intercamp except as scorekeepers and will never play a high school sport. Kids who spend their time with their heads in books and comic books. Dreamers. And though both Corey and I were camp and college athletes, we both have more than a little bit of dreamer in us. And we both love my father. See versions of ourselves in him. Know that, in spite of all the John Wayne bravado, he's at heart a guy who loves books and music and poetry. Who has advanced degrees in English and Counseling. Who acted and sang in all the end-of-the-summer musicals. At his best, a sheep in wolf's clothing.

*

One of my most treasured childhood memories is of my father singing "I Got Life," from *Hair*, staged on the painted green basketball court of the rec hall, the first Marc Jacobs production of what would become a nearly two-decade-long tradition of end-of-the-summer musicals. I couldn't have been more than eight years old and I don't think I've ever seen a video or heard a recording of it, but I remember my movie-star handsome father dancing in a tie-dye shirt and jeans in front of hundreds of laughing and cheering campers and counselors, not missing a step or a note: "I got life, Mother. I got laughs, Sister. I got freedom, Brother" and I remember how much in awe I was of the sheer communal joy of it, and then the roar of the crowd when he turned his back to all of us, bent at the waist and sang out "I GOT MY ASS." He was fantastic.

Most of my happiest memories with my father involve music. I've always believed that my father was an athlete with an artist's soul. He married a ballet dancer and an actress and was always quoting poetry, dancing around the living room, or singing along to the radio, especially at Christmas time, when Elvis, Nat King Cole, and Frank Sinatra dominated the airwaves. I used to love going Christmas tree shopping with him, driving down Route 1 from one brightly lit lot to another, trying to find the perfect tree for the lowest price, lights flashing in the falling snow as my father sang about the little drummer boy, chestnuts roasting on an open fire and how wonderful the world would be "if every day could be just like Christmas." Even when my grandfather was dying of Alzheimer's Disease there was something achingly beautiful about the drives my father and I took to the nursing home and back, the dial always set on Oldies 103, my father crooning along in a rich baritone better than the King's.

*

It's Corey who finally tells me I need to start going to the meetings again. "You need to be there, man. He's better when you're around. More focused. Less volatile, you know." So I get my ass out of bed, pull on a white t-shirt and jeans, grab a cup of ashy coffee from the dining hall and zombie my way down the hill, tasked with keeping an eye on my father, anticipating little explosions, pulling him aside or putting a hand on his back when I think he might be ready to pop off. Redirecting him: "didn't you want me to help set up the nets for European Handball this morning?" It doesn't always work. He may have memory problems, but he isn't stupid. "Since when did you start coming to these things" he snapped at me one day, "What are you now, my babysitter? What? So now I need my son to keep an eye on me?"

I've often said to my mother and to my sisters that my father's dementia, his memory loss, is "a" problem" but his anger is "*the*" problem. The truth is, of course, that they are bound up in one another (one reason both Corey and I have been advocating for anti-depressant or anti-anxiety medication). Medical professionals have told my mother that anger is common to those who suffer memory loss—especially those, like my father, whose identity is bound up in control, power, or intellect. Long before my father began showing signs of dementia, I had become fixated on the connection between memory and identity and, more generally, what makes a person. Watching my grandfather disappear into Alzheimer's as a young boy created a dread of forgetting, an uncomfortable holding of the breath whenever my father couldn't find his reading glasses or his keys, that is mirrored in my household—where my frantic searches for my phone, my laptop, and my coffee mug, touch off little panic attacks that leave Rachael and Darius caught between trying to help me and give me space. The brain injuries I suffered both from football as a boy (four concussions) and the accident have only turned those anxieties into an obsession, given fuel when I became a writer whose work depended so much on memory. Over the years, books exploring the scientific and philosophical implications of identity, memory, dementia, the mind and how it works have piled on my desk and shelves, stacked and scattered among my other obsessions—*The Identities of Persons, Losing My Mind, How the Mind Works, The Man Who Mistook His Wife for a Hat, Of Personal Identity* sharing space with Rumi, Toni Morrison, William Faulkner, and dozens of fantasy novels, poetry collections, and biographies of artists and musicians.

What I have discovered is that there is a great deal of argument about whether personhood is a product of memory. My experiences with my father support Oliver Sacks's belief that even someone with advanced dementia retains "aspects of [his or her] essential character, of personality and personhood, of self" that "survive—along with certain, almost indestructible forms of memory."[1] My father is still there. Even his angry outbursts are nothing new—just more frequent and less connected to obvious triggers. For someone like my father, what's happening to him is about much more than memory. His rage is a reaction to fear, fear of losing his sense of self—the one that he has built over the years and has been reflected by others throughout his life, what Rousseau called the amour propre—that vision of oneself that is affirmed by the esteem of others. So who we are is indistinguishable from how we are seen. For the first sixty-five years of his life my father was the smartest, best-looking, most talented, most respected, most feared, most important person in the room, no matter what room he was in. He didn't just know the schedule; he made the schedule. To be laughed at. To need help. To need to be reminded of how many outs there are in a game or what inning it is or be pulled back to the bench by a frantic assistant as he heads out to the mound because he doesn't realize it is his second trip, to be ignored, to simply not be that important—is to not be Joel Peckham. What is left is as raw and fragile as an exposed nerve.

  On a rational level I know that his explosions are beyond his control, are amplified by that very sense of being out of control. This is not a directed fury but something existential and desperate. And yet I sometimes struggle to be patient, to have sympathy because his anger is not new to me. I recognize it as one of those essential aspects of his personality and can't help but see his outbursts as a matter of character, not illness. Demons, not dementia. And the feeling I am having of just wanting to walk away from him, to get away, to hide from him is engrained and familiar. His anger working its frequency into me, so I am buzzing with it.

  I resent it.

  Anger has always been the problem. I love my father. I'm afraid of my father. He is a beautiful, sensitive, passionate man—even in his late seventies, his once jet-black hair turning silver, his eyes an icy blue. And he is surprisingly strong for a relatively small person—just a shade over 5'8" and smaller since a hip replacement changed his posture and gait from an upright stride to a hunched shuffle. To put a hand on his back or shoulder is to encounter knots of hard muscle. There's a coiled intensity to him. This is also part of his beauty and force. We might all laugh at his threat to punch Waldo, but I'm still pretty sure that if he decided to do so, the laughter would stop. Quickly. He loves fiercely too. And often he struggles to know the difference between rage and passion. He believes in simple values like loyalty, perseverance, and integrity. But the universe has always had him at the center and so he has learned to separate everyone around him into allies and enemies. "I don't trust that guy," he tells me, eyes narrowing in the shadow of his cap, "he thinks he's hot shit." Which is another way of saying, *that guy doesn't come to me for advice anymore, that guy thinks he's more important than I am.* What he can't face is that he really has no enemies here. Or allies, really. That he's just not on the radar.

"You don't understand," he says, hammering both fists down on the railing in front of him. "No one listens to me. I'm just the village idiot. They're all laughing at me behind my back. They don't let me do anything." He pauses for a moment—almost long enough for me to wonder if he has lost track of what he was saying. I could step into this silence, try to redirect him to other concerns. Or I could try reminding him of how beloved he is here, a legend really.

And that's true. My father is part of the lore of this place and his name and legacy is literally stamped on it. But it is also true that yes, when he threatens to punch Waldo, or gets caught in a loop where he just keeps repeating the same sentence as if it were a brand-new idea, people laugh at him. Sometimes out of discomfort, sometimes out of the simple callous and casual cruelty that can be a part of this place. Its humor a kind of stabbing irony. And I think that what he is struggling with the most right now is not that anyone in particular is doing anything to him, but that increasingly, it's not about him. That he doesn't matter anymore. That no one sees him. And when they do it's as a senile and comically grumpy old man.

I could tell him that I know exactly what it feels like to not be listened to.

I run a music program at a sports camp.

But I resent having to listen to him complain. I don't have a legacy to lose. And so I have a hard time sympathizing and I recoil at his fury. I want to tell him to just let it go. That it doesn't really matter, that his pride, his refusal to let go, is killing him and driving the rest of us crazy. That I just want to think about my program, my campers, my staff. I want to walk across the tennis courts, up the steps into the back of the rec hall, into the band room, count off the intro, strum an E7 and just tear into a song with my friends, until we find that moment where nothing else in the world matters but the roar of a distorted guitar, the throb of a bass and one voice coming together with another voice and then a third, until I'm not anyone or anywhere but disappear into the song. Freedom lives there.

Instead, I look straight into his blue eyes and pull him into a hug. "I just don't know why I'm here anymore," he says, "they don't know . . I don't know . . . who I am anymore." Beneath my feet I can feel the building vibrate with hundreds of footsteps. Benches groan across a concrete floor. And I don't care that everyone in camp can see us through the window. Or that any second now we will be swept along as a thousand little feet come streaming through the doors. I'm just a son holding onto his father, saying, "I know, Dad. I know."

*

It has been a hard summer for rhythm. Hard to find the one—that first beat in the measure when everyone needs to come back in, on time. Without Rachael and Darius, my days feel aimless and uncertain. I'm not sleeping well, going to bed later and later. Drinking too much bourbon, smoking too much weed, waiting to lie down until I'm so wiped out I can't avoid sleep. Until I'm certain it will slam into me like a train. Then I'll be out, fitfully dreaming for five to six hours before the sun pours into the cabin, my eyes fluttering open, and I roll out of bed to start it all over again. Everything reminds me of Rachael—from the paper lantern hanging from the rafters to the vintage, blue-velvet fold-out couch we purchased at a consignment shop, to the tall blue bookcases, to the sail-like sheet draped along the ceiling. All speaking to her eye for design. Her nearly absurd attempt to give this place a sense of home. The cabin itself is literally sunk several feet into an overgrown gully, what in West Virginia we'd call a holler, that sits in the shadows between Alumni Hall, a large indoor basketball facility on one side and the dining hall on the other. I have no idea how long the building has stood, but it has been here as long as I can remember. At one time, back when the kitchen staff was made up of BUNAC workers, blue collar Brits who took the job for free air fare and the opportunity see the states, the building served as a waiter's cabin, its one large room and single bathroom and shower housing twelve men. On exposed rafter beams you can still see the graffiti. Bill was here in 1979. Tom slept here in 1975. Now, partitioned into two living spaces by a thin barrier of particleboard that runs down the center of the cabin, it serves as director's housing for me on one side and my friend Scotty Perrin, the lacrosse director, on the other. The entire structure leans just enough so that one corner of the roof hangs out over the road a crucial few inches, causing food trucks and busses to misjudge the sharp turn striking the cabin and setting the place to swaying and lurching like a boat on a wave of dust. When Rach first came to camp, she found the rustic quality of cabin life charming. She grew up on a pig farm in Michigan and was unbothered by bugs or dirt or mold. But over time its charm wore off. She tried to add a little class to the place over thirteen years, purchasing furniture, and a heavy wooden screen to create a sort of bedroom, separate from the living space. And by camp standards, we lived in luxury. But whatever we bought would have to sit in place for ten months, subject to the elements and any rodents who found a way through the walls' and floors' many cracks and holes to burrow their way into a mattress, a couch cushion, or a chest of drawers. For years I wouldn't even let Rach enter the cabin until I had first examined it for dead rats and live squirrels. But after thirteen years of coming to camp with me, our son, Darius, and our Golden Retrievers, she and Darius finally decided enough was enough. Rachael missed her house, her bed, and her freedom away from bugle calls, communal meals, the dust and noise of food trucks arriving at 6am, or buses rolling in at 11pm, and the flood of testosterone everywhere. And Darius wanted to have one summer with his high school friends before starting college. "I fully support you going," Rach told me. "But I'm done." Still, I don't think she really expected me to take her up on her suggestion that I come back alone. Especially this year.

*

Even on the first day of orientation, when I'd completed the sixteen-hour drive, parked the Corolla and started the walk down the hill toward the office, I felt a desperate need to leave. Every other summer this had been one of the high points of my year. I would come up early, ahead of Rachael and Darius, our dog, Ivy, spinning in circles in the back seat as she recognized the downward slope of highway, the canopy of trees opening up into ball fields and basketball courts. From the top of the hill, you can see all the way to East Pond, a large glacial lake on the Belgrade chain, rippling flat and blue, stretching out toward Birch Island and the northern Appalachian mountains beyond. I'd stop in front of our cabin and let Ivy explode from the car, sprinting first to the porch of my parents' cabin at the bottom of the hill, to find it empty (they always arrived a little late to orientation) and then down to the waterfront. I'd follow Ivy slowly, taking my time, breathing in the scent of mud and saturated wood, pine and sap, letting each stone and daylily trigger decades of memory. Allowing old friends to recognize me, calling out the cartoonish and absurd nickname I wear in this place, JPJ (Joel Peckham Junior) and jogging up to give me a hug. I had moved so many times. Lived in ten different states, four apartments, and five houses. Held jobs at four different universities and a private high school. And for a long time, this was the closest thing I had to a home. The one constant in my life that often felt broken between so many befores and afters. Manitou was always there. An essential part of who I was and am.

But this summer I've just felt lost, confused, and on the verge of tears every moment. So when I sat down with David Schiff on the second floor of the office building, the place alive with ringing phones, the walls packed to the ceiling with duffle bags and sports equipment, I found myself unable to muster any warmth or enthusiasm at all. I sat there, looking around at the building that I still considered new, 20 years after it had been built, thinking of the old office (now the radio room and counselor lounge) and how I'd run through it as a little boy, chased by Jill, an overwhelmed and apologizing babysitter, my swim trunks in one hand, my sister Tina pulled along in the other.

I knew exactly where they kept the best candy for "canteen" and the best toys from the lost and found, both sharing a long, dark corridor walled with cubby holes on either side, masking tape labels announcing "Charleston Chew," "Twizzler," "M&M's," "Flashlights," "Batteries." There were baskets of fishing rods and nerf footballs, contraband squirt guns and jackknives (confiscated from deep in some child's duffle bag). At the beginning of every summer, my mother and I would rifle through clothes that no one had ever claimed the previous season—not only camp apparel but sports equipment, books, and electronics. We'd check for names or tags and if the camper was no longer on the list of returning boys, she'd black the name out with a sharpie and write mine in its place. It never bothered me that so much of what I owned was secondhand. That I was wearing some rich kid's clothes. It never occurred to me, really, because in a cabin where everyone had to follow the same rules, those class distinctions were easy to ignore. No one ever said anything about the fact that my shirts and shorts were always too big or too tight. The only time I felt the difference was on visiting day when I'd watch the expensive and exotic cars roll into camp, and then watch mothers and stepmothers navigate the hills and ball fields in crazy high heels and outfits intended more for an expensive resort than a summer camp. As I combed through lost treasure I could hear my father's booming voice, gravelly even then, upbraiding some counselor who was "dumb as wood" or "didn't know his ass from his elbow" in the back room where he sat at a large circular table that made me think of Camelot. It was either a privilege or a terror to be called "to the back of the office" over the PA, depending on what my father wanted to speak to you about. I was not allowed in that room most of the time, so I'd avoid it, sometimes poking my head into the office of Uncle Bobby Marcus, a long-limbed young man still, though prematurely balding with a terrible comb-over. He had just purchased the camp from his older brother, who had inherited it from his father and seemed caught between the shock and joy of the responsibility. Always on the verge of laughing or screaming, eyes bulging like Marty Feldman's. "Jo Jo, what are you up to now, you little knucklehead, yooou idiot."

  I loved him.

  Back when Uncle Bobby was just a photography counselor, he used to lope down to our little suite of rooms in the large moldy fishing lodge by the lake, a guitar slung across his back so he could sing "Drunken Sailor," "Zoom Gully Gully," and "Puff the Magic Dragon" to us before we went to bed. My sisters, Lisa and Tina, would beg him to "please stop" and would crawl all over him as he fumbled with the chords and laughed. My sisters tell me he had a terrible voice, but I don't remember it that way. I just remember thinking that "Puff the Magic Dragon" was the greatest, sweetest, saddest, song I'd ever heard.

  And I stared at Dave Schiff and thought about how long I'd known him, remembering clearly the eleven-year-old boy I'd coached in baseball my first summer as a counselor when I was seventeen years old—that same bushy shock of hair gray now, peppered throughout. And how my friend Feldy and I decided we'd put him on the team if he could just catch a single pop fly. He didn't. We took him anyway. And I thought about all the friends and family I had seen come and go from this place. Not only people who had moved on, but who had died. The directors and campers and counselors who had passed through this place in the 49 years since my father first showed up to direct the athletic program, a not yet thirty-year-old high school English teacher with a young wife, two little girls and a baby boy on the way. So many names and faces that they had begun to blur and blend. And I thought about how this was the last summer any of us would be here. I felt sad. Exhausted. Ashamed. Old. And I couldn't get the lyrics about Jackie Paper leaving Puff out of my head and the great silence of the dragon that leads us back into the chorus.

Dave chattered excitedly about the summer, about camp, about the great staff I had. "It's an A+ program, Joel. You've done a great job. We have big plans. And next year . . . ." I cut him off mid-sentence. "Dave, I need to be honest with you. I'm not sure if I should be here and I'm not sure if I can stay. I could leave at any time. I might not still be here by dinner." He nodded—a little stunned. I had told him about Rachael and the biopsy on a phone call a month before, "just to keep him in the loop." And I told him that if it came back clean, I would head on up to camp, but if it didn't, he'd need to replace me. So when the report came back benign, we celebrated for an hour and then I got in the car and drove to Maine. But it felt wrong. The ache in my gut and the pressure in my chest as I drove through the mountains out of West Virginia told me something fundamental was changing in my life, and very soon, but sitting there in that office, miles away from Rachael and Darius, I had the feeling that maybe it already had and I had just been too slow to recognize it—or had refused to. "I thought you should know." There was a little bit of silence.

"OK. Well, let's see how it goes."

*

When the weather is good, Manitou's schedule appears to be a rigid one, each day beginning with breakfast, then a cleanup period, followed by inspection of the cabins and then three periods of "instructionals" before lunch. Instructionals are intended as opportunities for the kids to learn a new skill or to practice and refine old ones. For almost fifty years, Manitou's instructional program has been one of the best in camping and one of the key draws for parents who send their kids away in the summer in hopes that they may return stronger, healthier, and more mature—with better social skills and maybe a few lifelong friends. For decades the self-improvement ethos was stitched into the DNA of nearly all the boys and girls summer camps that sprang up throughout New England in the first decades of the twentieth century. Most of these camps had Jewish affiliations and were an attempt to give kids from urban communities a chance to get some fresh air and experience their community in a setting that was immersive and safe from the pervasive antisemitism that surrounded them. Henry Marcus founded Manitou in 1947 at a time when the memories of Hitler youth were very fresh in the consciousness of the community. B'nai B'rith's slogan "NEVER AGAIN" was not simply a call to political action but for a change in community—one that prioritized unity, self-sufficiency, and strength.

With time, however, that ethos has changed, and the instructional program has suffered for it—part a product of the massive expansion in camper numbers, part a shift in demographics and culture. The camp's religious affiliation, never a strict one, has eroded. Up until the early eighties the entire camp would still gather for Friday night services in the Rec Hall. Auntie Sue Marcus would preside on stage, standing thin and elegant behind a lectern, her hair cropped short like a 1920s flapper. There were candles lit, a short prayer, and then her arms would rise along with her sonorous "Good Shabbos."

"Good Shabbos," we would chant back. Then copies of a mimeographed service booklet of songs and prayers would circulate among the benches. "Puff the Magic Dragon" was in there along with several other folk songs and pop tunes that were growing dusty even then: "If I Had a Hammer," "Kumbaya," "Peace Train," "Let it Be," "Morning has Broken," as well as quite a few spirituals, including "Michael Row the Boat Ashore" and my favorite, "Swing Low, Sweet Chariot" (which the older boys would perform with irreverent hand gestures emphasizing the word "coming" each time it appeared in the chorus). These were sung with the combination of enthusiasm, expertise, and sincerity one might expect from a mass choir made up of two hundred Jewish boys being forced to sing folk songs and spirituals, not a few of whom were going through hormonal changes, and very few of whom were making an effort to hit the notes or find the pitch.

I tried. I always tried. I loved to sing and had a good, if girlish, tenor. I even played around with harmony sometimes. And, lost among so many voices, I felt safe to try. After the songs, selected counselors, still in their very short shorts and high tube socks, their hair long, with bushy mustaches and sideburns that would have made Elvis jealous, would rise from the benches to speak about their experiences working with the Peace Corps, building houses for the homeless, or their time spent living on a kibbutz in Israel. I vividly remember Andy Arenson, then the Archery instructor, talking about killing chickens by grabbing them by the heads and beaks and spinning them in wide arcs until the necks snapped or the bodies separated completely in a spray of blood—and how when the birds were set back down, they would run around for a while, aimless and senseless. A story that gave me nightmares.

But the highlight of the evening was always the achievement badges awarded at the very end of the service, handed out by various heads of instructionals and intercamp teams. Campers' names would be called out and boys would walk up to applaud for accomplishments in everything from marksmanship to track, swimming, skiing, and acting. I sometimes wonder what happened to my little collection of badges, once stashed in the small underwear drawer in my room in Sharon, Massachusetts. I did search for them once in a fit of nostalgia, ransacking the house. They probably sit in some cardboard box, buried in a dusty corner of the laundry room or maybe the attic.

As the camp has skewed younger, and parenting attitudes have changed, the old-school ethic focusing on the value of hard work, internal motivation, and community has changed as well to a more consumer-based ethic built around principles of individual choice and empowerment. There are still opportunities for competition, teamwork, and the learning of new skills, but the emphasis on fun and freedom has altered or erased many camp traditions. A camper in the 70s needed to accept the idea that much of the day he would be participating in activities he might not enjoy or even hated—like swim lessons in 55 degree lake water, pottery, or track—with the grudging understanding that their parents had signed them up for those activities and that occasionally, doing something you didn't want to do might be good for you. This is no longer the case. There are no services. No badges and not much incentive for campers to sign up for some of the more difficult or strenuous activities. If the day is hot and a camper doesn't want to go to baseball or football, he can head to a window outside of the office and change his assignment up to an hour before the period begins. As a result, our instructional lists are basically meaningless, and it can be difficult to keep track of the campers or to find them if they don't show up. The most popular instructionals are often the ones that require the least amount of effort. Radio, for example, which was at one time a serious learning instructional where campers were taught journalism and broadcasting required kids to use real radio equipment that sent their voices out to the city of Oakland and beyond, now involves about 20 campers sitting in a little room eating Icy-Pops while a counselor plays their music requests over the camp's outdoor PA system.

This sounds as if I am critiquing the change, but that's not exactly right. In fact, I imagine that as a child I would have liked this version of Manitou much better than the one I grew up in—one where every minute of my day was driven by competition and a relentless need to prove myself.

But the resulting environment of loosely controlled chaos is particularly confusing to my father. Routine is essential to those who struggle with dementia. Being able to rely on what comes next, to move through the day without surprises, can reduce much of the anxiety and frustration brought on when one struggles to retain information in the short term. That my father continues to have an excellent long-term memory can actually make a problem worse, since he will often forget about changes made in the program (and sometimes even the facility). As a result, he is not only resistant to change but suspicious and frightened of it—incapable of adjusting or adapting. At one time my father was in charge of most of what was going on at camp on any given day precisely because he was so adept at keeping almost every part of the camp program in his head at the same time. As his problems with memory have asserted themselves, however, his responsibilities have narrowed to running the baseball program, focusing most of his attention on the varsity team's intercamp practices, which usually occur during 2nd and 3rd periods.

It is not a matter of hyperbole to say that my father's baseball program is legendary in camping, so good for so long that there was a time when other camps refused to play us or would regularly try to sneak counselors onto their squads simply to make the games somewhat competitive. During one five-year period in the early 90s, the Manitou Varsity (15 and under) team ran off 33 consecutive wins, including several against local Legion baseball teams. One of the reasons the program continued to be dominant into the early 21st century was that parents believed their kids would get better training at Manitou than they could at camps and summer leagues specifically focused on baseball. Youth baseball is not a particularly exciting sport to watch, but on Visiting Days parents would crowd the bleachers, marveling at my father's knowledge, his charisma, and the incredibly efficient choreography of his coaching. Stunned by how readily their boys would do whatever he told them to do, bursting out of the dugout to sprint wherever he told them to go, hanging on to every word he said, impressed at how he could work with each child individually while keeping track of the many moving parts around him, his staff confident and capable, most of them ex-campers who knew all the drills and revered him like a God. Here, a group of kids practicing how to lay down a bunt at a whiffle ball machine. There, another group at the batting cages—one child hitting against the machine while others hit off tees and practiced "soft-toss," hitting lobbed baseballs into a net. Every child involved. Everyone doing exactly what he was supposed to do. Everyone knowing how to do it. But it has been years since my father could manage the program on his own.

Even on good days he can't remember the names of his players or which positions they play. He'll have them repeat the same drill over and over because he's lost track of the time he's spent on it. And he'll forget to cover essential elements of preparation that once distinguished his program from those at other camps—pick-off plays, first and third situations, knowing which cutoff man to throw to. So I'll try to set up my instructional so that I have one free period to help him and when I don't, I'll have one staff member work with the kids on a song, maybe another work with two kids on basic chord progressions or scales, then jog the twenty yards from the back of the Rec-Hall to Diamond #1 to see how my dad is doing, helping where I can, checking to make sure all of his staff have shown up, and speaking to them about how the day is going, putting out little fires as they erupt. (He left the list on his cart and his cart down at the flagpole. He blew up at one of his staff members for asking him where the list is, telling him "get your ass off my field." He has had the kids running bases for 30 minutes when it's 95 degrees out—not because he is trying to be cruel but because he has lost track of the time. He never showed up and no one knows where he is.)

I knew today was going to be stressful even before my father's meltdowns at the meeting and then at breakfast. There is a baseball tournament coming up and we don't know what we have for a team, Visiting Day is only one week away. As for me, I have an ambitious set planned with fifteen full-band numbers and several solo performances. Over twenty campers will perform in the show.

When I jog over to diamond number one, there are ten-year-olds who have been given nothing to do and are just sitting listlessly in the dugout, watching my very angry father try to run an infield outfield with only five players. One assistant coach is serving as catcher and another, a 17-year-old Junior Counselor, is sitting in the dugout with the kids, spitting sunflower seeds onto the concrete floor. When I jog up, he startles a bit. I may be the music director, but I'm still built like a linebacker, and he can tell I'm not happy with what I'm seeing. I am so used to being misinterpreted based on appearance that I sometimes lean into it, and this is one of those times. I consciously straighten my posture, crossing my arms over my chest. As a result of the accident, I suffer from chronic joint and nerve pain that causes me to clench my jaw—the resulting look is a hard one, unsmiling and grim. I almost feel sorry for the kid as he tries to explain the situation. Apparently, my father forgot that he had scheduled practice and so had forgotten to remind the players at breakfast.

This is not all my father's fault. That there are six junior campers assigned to third period instructional on a day when Varsity Baseball is having practice is symptomatic of 21st century Manitou. I'm sure that if I could find my father's list, each of these campers would have been late additions, having been moved over from somewhere else. Maybe there wasn't enough space on a ski-boat, or they put too many kids at the climbing tower. Half of the kids have shown up without gloves or hats. One is wearing flip-flops. My father shouldn't have to remind anyone about practice. His players should have been assigned baseball for instructional the week before the tournament (which is in three days). It should have been on their schedule, and they shouldn't have been allowed to change it. And this JC knows enough baseball to work with a small group by himself; he's just so used to my father telling him exactly what to do and when that when it didn't happen, he probably thought it was safer to just sit there and do nothing. So, instead, I have to tell him to grab the basket of lost gloves from the shed, take the little ones over to Peckham Park and teach them basic infielding technique. Instead, I have to jog down to the waterfront to pull the shortstop off the fishing rock, tell the waterfront director to signal my mother on the ski-boat to bring our starting pitcher in to shore, and then run over to radio to get the first baseman off the couch, into cleats and up the hill. I find the leftfielder taking a nap in the CIT cabin. I've had to talk most of these kids into playing in the first place, even recruiting a few musicians to fill out the roster. Because who wants to practice baseball in 90-degree heat when you could be out on the lake enjoying the breeze or eating an Icy Pop in an air-conditioned radio room.

The entire period is only forty-five minutes and I need to assemble a varsity baseball team, then get back to the band room to hear the final run-through of the song the kids are prepping for visiting day, so I am hustling, running around camp, up and down the hill, one end to the other, a 48-year old man covered in sweat, cursing and laughing the entire time, sprinting across basketball courts and shouting apologies to campers and coaches alike, half my brain on tracking down baseball players, the other half listening to the punk version of Elvis's "Suspicious Minds" I have somehow convinced our varsity band to play for their parents: it chugs along relentlessly, sounding, at least to me, much better than it did a couple of days ago, and light years better than whatever electronic dance music the "radio" program is trying to drown it out with. Steph and Eric have all three vocalists singing in something approaching harmony. The rhythm guitarist is playing the correct four chords in the correct order *and in time*. Our drummer, ironically, is on the baseball team and is one of the few players who showed up for practice, so Julia is sitting in on the kit, but I know Noah can handle the part. I love Noah. The lead guitar is our problem this year. I've told our guitar instructor, Ethan, that Jake has three days to get his solo down or we'll have to pull it. And though I know that it would be a relief to both the band and the staff, especially Ethan, if I would do just that (*Joel, not every song has to have a solo*), they are trying very hard to get him where he needs to be. I am amused by Ethan's struggles with Jake, a kind of Karmic whiplash that keeps me believing in a balanced universe. Ethan has been part of the program since he was nine years old, and was pulled into the band for being moderately talented and insanely adorable with huge brown eyes and good hair. He was also hopelessly ADHD and either missed or was late to almost every band practice we ever had. I have uttered the phrase "where the fuck is Ethan Gale" so many times over the past decade, that former staff members will randomly splice it into conversations when they call to wish me happy birthday, or to simply catch up. And still, I love Ethan. I've always loved Ethan. And he's become a wonderful staff member, especially when working with kids like Jake who *never* forgets about practice, but cannot follow directions otherwise. Who pointlessly noodles on his guitar when people are trying to talk ("he's not even playing scales, Joel, just random notes"). Our most important show is a week away, in front of parents. Ethan has already snapped at Jake, "if you play that guitar one more time while I'm trying to talk, I swear I'll shove it up your ass." Which only resulted in everyone in the band room, including Jake, collapsing into fits of laughter.

  We all want the show to be great. Unreasonably so. It's one of only two days at camp where what we do *matters*. When we have an audience that is actively listening. Our show, once a ten-minute burst of noise played on bad equipment on the Rec Hall floor, has gotten better each year with better singers and performances, better quality instruments, and more complicated and difficult songs and arrangements. The previous summer the campers covered Fleetwood Mac's "The Chain" and a parent recorded it on his phone, then texted the file to his friend, Lindsey Buckingham. After the set, the excited father showed me the response—"sounds pretty great." We were ecstatic.

*

It is more than ironic that I find myself so frustrated by—and victim of—such a breakdown in the camp's once rigid and predictable organization. For one thing, I couldn't run my program at a camp that required its campers to actually be where they are supposed to be all the time. You can't teach music during three forty-five-minute instructional periods stretched out over one week. And you certainly can't pull a band together that way. My musicians—campers and staff—are nearly always in the band room, sometimes practicing with each other, sometimes by themselves, during rest periods, free swims, and late at night. Like me, they've learned to find the spaces in the schedule. They have learned how to make space for themselves here.

But I am also almost incapable of functioning within a rigidly defined system. I often think that much of the tension between me and my father as I grew up was due to my fundamental inability to do anything according to directions. Attention deficit before such a thing was an entry in the DSM and before treatments like Ritalin or Adderall were dispensed *en masse* to inattentive and hyperactive young boys along with their pop tarts and orange juice, I was the glassy-eyed kid who was never where he was supposed to be or when. The one who lost all of his textbooks the first week of school, who was as likely to have a baseball bounce off his head out in right field as he was to catch it, who constantly left his lunch on the bus, and who was routinely punished for staring out the window during class, distracted by a bird, or the rain, or a cloud in the shape of a bird, or just some song about rain that was stuck in his head. "I know *that* he's thinking," a sympathetic, if exasperated, teacher once told my parents, "I just don't know what about." Of his three children, I was the one my father had the most difficulty understanding, the one he struggled the most to mentor. My report cards would come home, and I would sit in the living room with my mother as he towered over me, shouting and waving his arms violently through the air, as if by speaking louder he could get through to me, the way some Americans will raise their voices when trying to communicate with non-English speakers. How can you be getting a "D" in *English* and an "F" in *History*? All you *do* is read!"

*

I am an associative thinker, and my memories are episodic. As a consequence, I tend not to see or understand my life in terms of cause and effect but relationally—through how one moment may connect me to another. So my sense of time has less to do with duration than it does to pattern, rhythm, and tempo. I make meaning through seeking out connections. In fact, I distrust memory—and not just because of the experiences of my father and grandfather. Not just because I feel a chill whenever a name or a lyric or a word doesn't leap to mind—one that has always been there but now seems buried in storage in an unlabeled bin or lost in a field of static. And I think *Has it started? Is this the beginning?* Even if I didn't have a genetic predisposition to dementia, I would consider memory a shaky foundation on which to build personhood. Socrates, and Locke after him, comes very near to equating memory with consciousness and argues that our identity cannot be separated from our ability to process and retain ideas and experiences. Locke spends most of his *Essay Concerning Human Understanding* untangling the implications of this idea. For example, if a man does not remember having committed a crime, if he has no recollection of it, can he be held accountable for that action? Locke's answer is something of an equivocation—he can be judged by man but not by God.[2] Which sounds absurd and yet this argument is a common one. As Locke points out, we often excuse a person's behavior because "he was not himself" or was "beside himself," and what is "temporary insanity" if not a means of separating man from person. The action from the identity. When my father hits my mother in the middle of the night while under the influence of a vivid nightmare and then has no memory of it the next morning, can he be held accountable for assault? My mother certainly doesn't think so. Most mornings she won't even tell him about it. "What is the point? He says it never happened and if I show him the bruises, he just breaks down. He's inconsolable." I've often wondered if selective memory may be a kind of self-defense. How do we process an action that does not fit into our self-perception? What if we can't bear to look at the images from the past, what if we bury it, or lock it away?

For many years after the accident, I traveled from state to state with belongings that I could not fit into a two-bedroom apartment or didn't trust to the moldy basements and attics of a rental home. The solution was a low-rent storage facility, usually Bob's or Bill's, or Larry's, usually a mile or two off an interstate. Sometimes I would visit just to check on things, pulling into the lot and dragging up the rattling door to stare into a dark cubicle packed full of furniture, a bedframe, a piano, boxes of Cyrus's school projects. I didn't really want to take anything home. I just wanted to know that it was still there. Waiting for me when I was ready for it. In the end I gave almost all of it away to Goodwill. Though there are still a few items that have traveled with me. The large plastic box of Cyrus's spelling and math books, art supplies, and drawings will come with me wherever I go. Someday I will open it.

But memory is not just a storage facility waiting for us to punch in the right codes for access. Whatever waits for us in its boxes and safes must still be stitched together. It is a construct, and we make up the pattern as we go. As a writer of nonfiction, I have simply encountered too much variance in how people remember events, too much fluidity in how memories are shaped, and too much fallibility in the process of how we shape narratives and meaning from what we recall to trust anyone's story of the past as reliable, especially my own. So much can get in the way. The mind tends to manipulate events, especially in terms of time, shuffling experiences from different days, months, or years, moving things closer together or further apart or superimposing them one on the other. Filling gaps to explain the relationship of events, or to create causes and effects that lend purpose and meaning to experience, to place it in a context intended to help us to see it more clearly. In reality, all we manage to do is process the experience and images differently. We see the past through another lens, in another way. We justify an action only in retrospect. We align our pasts and our intentions to fit the image we have of ourselves. Only we do not know ourselves. And maybe we don't really want to know.

After telling a close friend that I had been having lucid dreams, she advised me to try to take control of them. "If possible, look in a mirror. I've heard that if you do, you see yourself for who you really are." I remember nodding silently and thinking, *who would ever actually do that? What could be more terrifying?*

Even when we are trying our best to tell a true story, our intentions, our view of ourselves, our need to impose meaning, our capacity for self-deception, get in the way. In my creative nonfiction classes we have long discussions about how truthful, how honest we need to be. My answer is that we should honor the contract with the reader, to tell the truth, to the best of our ability. Which is almost an admission of that task's impossibility. To fabricate is not to lie, to create is not to dissemble, to re-create is not to obscure actual events—not exactly. The intentions of art, the ethics of the storyteller and the essayist, exist in a world without easy binaries. There is no choice but to fabricate. How an artist makes meaning of the past only takes us further down a road of ordering and meaning-making that began before the writing started—with the unconscious process of taking the information the brain receives from the eyes and nose and ears, tastebuds, and fingertips and then *processing it* all across its various lobes, cortexes and synapses of the brain. For example, recent studies of how the brain receives information from the eyes suggest that what we see as a unified image of the world is based on startlingly little actual data. There are huge gaps that the brain has to leap across in order to construct an image. The reorganization of this material into something meaningful is essential to both the artistic process and the process of memory formation. But it is only one, highly processed vision and version of the world.

    And writers are constantly making choices regarding what gets left in and left out of the picture (not to mention how and where and what will be framed). And there is always a certain amount of gap-filling. Once the process of narrating begins, it can become very difficult to untangle the actual and authentic from the fabricated. Often, I have a great deal of trouble deciding if I am recollecting what happened or if I am inventing it. And we have all experienced what happens when two or three people recollect an event to each other: very quickly the conversation will turn into an argument regarding who has the most authentic story-- "that never happened" or "that happened but" it was on a different day, a different year, with different people. "We didn't have the Chevy yet. It was Volkswagen bus and it wasn't orange, it was red. And we never would have let you sleep in the back without seatbelts." "But the Volkwagen didn't have seatbelts." "What happened to the Chevy anyway?" Of course, how we remember, what we remember, and why we remember it has everything to do with identity. We are all the center of our own universes, the heroes of our stories. Perspective changes everything—especially in terms of the stakes. When someone challenges your memory, it can feel like something vital to you is under threat—because it is. We may or may not be our memories, but much of who we are and what we think about ourselves is based on our processing and retention of experience: we are the stories we tell ourselves about ourselves. We are the arrangement of the notes, the chords, we are the composition.

*

The band room, or as my staff and campers refer to it, The Room, is actually our second iteration of the practice room, though in some ways the move to the new space was a return as much as it was a new beginning. After seven years and several aborted promises from the owners to build us our own facility, we were relocated to the back room of the Rec Hall—a space that had the advantage of being in the same building where our Visiting Day show took place and was also only a dozen yards away from Diamond #1. "Now you won't have to run halfway across camp to help your dad," Dave said. I suspected even then that the real reason for our move had more to do with my stubborn refusal to turn down the amplifiers during basketball games and practices (and also with the *way* I refused: "get the fuck out of my band room!"), than with location, but I rolled with it, using the move as an excuse to upgrade our equipment. I also liked the fact that the new space was built on top of the original stage that once housed the theater program where I first learned to sing and perform in front of an audience. And I especially liked the fact that whenever we played, people would hear us all over camp. I gleefully packed up all the equipment, our fabric, our egg crates, loaded them into the back of a pick-up truck and drove it across the picnic area through right field and over to the Rec Hall. I felt like I had been handed the biggest boombox in the world. And I couldn't wait to plug it in and turn it up to 11.

The first year of the program, we were housed in Alumni Hall—the largest indoor facility at Manitou. Built in the 2000s, Robert Marcus Alumni Hall was essentially an airplane hangar modified to house a full-size basketball court, an indoor batting cage and weight room, as well as athletic offices and several "Rec Rooms."

The music program was assigned "Rec Room 1." As a music space, it was less than ideal. The surface of the basketball court was made up of parquet squares that "floated" above a poured concrete surface. But "floated" is the correct word in more ways than one. The large garage doors along the west wall were not water-tight, so when torrential storms inevitably buffeted our lakeside property, water would stream in, traveling in rivers beneath the court, and emptying out right at our door, soaking the carpet (a problem when you are using multiple extension cords and surge protectors to run five amps and a PA into two ungrounded wall sockets). The danger of possible electrocution wasn't even our main concern. We mostly joked about that. The real problem was that the walls of the room and ceiling were pine paneled and the floor was lightly carpeted concrete. This looked rustic and smelled wonderful. But the resulting acoustics bordered on dangerous.

I remember the first time I tried to run a practice with my new music staff, Davis McGraw and John Salvage on lead and bass, respectively, and Tristan Hewett—a talented Australian we borrowed from the waterfront—playing the wobbly old kit we'd salvaged from beneath the stage of the theater building. We tore through "Have Love Will Travel" by the Sonics, and the sound we produced in that echo chamber, bass-heavy and driven full blast through our pawn-shop amps and equipment was like a jet taking off. At that point in my life, I had played music with other people only one or two times and it was fun, but this was something else—hard charging, alive, distorted, and loud as hell. I knew I was a lousy guitarist, but I could sing a little and so could Davis and John. And if my acoustic-electric, running through the PA, was lost in the mix, all the better. I could feel the music vibrating all along my body as I flailed at the strings and screamed away. My nerve pain disappeared and the darkness pushed back—and for a few minutes I was a kid again, singing along with my family in my father's cavalier with the volume turned all the way up —a version of myself that wasn't about grief or loss, not because my grief was gone or because I was ignoring or avoiding it, but because it stopped being the center of my consciousness, that hard black stone was particalized and charged with electricity, lit in the glorious noise we were making and out of which we are made.

    I loved being lost in the mix.

    What I didn't love was the ringing in my ears that persisted for the next 24 hours, or the concern on Rachael's face when I kept asking her to repeat what she was saying. So Davis, John, and I took a trip to Mardens (think K-mart with a thick Maine accent) and bought several bolts of heavy paisley fabric then stole all the eggcrate we could find from mattresses throughout the empty cabins. And while Davis, John, and Tristan played orientation games, trying and failing to integrate with 150 jocks and frat-boys, I got a staple gun and got to work soundproofing the room. When I was done, its whorls of bordeaux, green, and gold seemed perfectly appropriate to the garage and psychedelic rock we were playing, and completely inappropriate to anything else in camp. As if someone had set up a band room in the front parlor of the House of the Rising Sun. And then moved the whole thing into your local YMCA. As I was putting the last staple into the ceiling Derek Worley walked in, staring first at the modified sign above the door—now "ROCK Room 1" (there was no ROCK Room 2) and then staring at the walls and ceiling in disbelief, laughing, shaking his head. "You know we have parents showing up in a few days, right? I'm guessing you didn't clear this with JD or Schiff." I handed him a beer and smiled, "So you like it then? Grab a mic. I need to do a sound check."

*

When I finally walk back into the band room, dragging Noah behind me, still in cleats, drumsticks and catcher's mitt clutched to his belly, there are only ten to fifteen minutes before Recall, the last bugle before lunch when the kids are supposed to report back to their cabins, take off wet suits and sports gear and wash up for the afternoon meal. I have grabbed Noah just as practice was ending and before my father sent the team (now at least eleven players strong) back to the dugout to go over signals (which he will forget, so I have already asked two players to write them down for me) and remind them to be there *on time* for practice the next morning (which I will need to remind him about during the morning meeting and again at breakfast).

I do not need to chase my musicians down. Noah even had his sticks in his catcher's bag. And though the entire camp is already in the process of heading down to the cabins, I can tell that no one in my program will leave until they have to. That every camper and staff member will stay until I flip the switch on the PA, waving them out the door and off to lunch. And chances are good that Eric will hang around even then, helping me to throw away spare coffee cups, power everything off, place capos and tuners in their proper drawers, and hang guitars on their hooks. And Julia and Steph will save us seats at a table for lunch. When I walk up the steps and into the back entrance under the Rock Room 1 sign (there is still no Rock Room 2), Steph is in the green room, a small entryway that we've soundproofed with more of this camp's seemingly endless supply of eggcrate and some green fabric DT salvaged from the last room—working on vocals with our three singers. Her smile flashes wide, giving me that raised eyebrow look of hers that tells me she's been up to something. The campers surrounding her, Max, Alex, and Hudson, are a strange looking group. Hudson is tall and blond with blunt bangs, a thick boned man-child with a deep voice. Alex is thinner, darker, with a large mouth full of braces and wiry black hair. His mannerisms are as delicate as his bone structure, but he can growl or croon and hit any note on the scale. They both tower over Maxwell, a very tan, very tiny 11-year-old who in a couple of years will be playing a lead role in the London stage production of School of Rock. But for right now, he's just Maxwell Apple (a.k.a. Mapple)—the kid who loves ACDC and sings the best version of TNT this side of Bon Scott. And he's adorable to boot. "You guys ready?" she asks them, and they nod. When we step into the band room, we are confronted with a happy, nervy, colorful, arrhythmic, discordant chaos. Jake is plucking random notes on a bass while sitting on an amp as DT attempts to go over his part. Eric is going over chords on the keyboard with Alex (whom we've renamed The Mad Russian because he lives in Moscow and speaks very little English).

Julia jumps up from the kit, pulling Noah into a hug. Everyone is smiling—except for Ethan, who really does look as if he's going to murder Jake. He won't, of course. Because we all love the kids. And we love our jobs.

It's been a long time since I've had to worry about leaving a staff member in charge of a practice. Any one of them could run the program and at different times, every one of them has. When I can't be there for a period, which is too often these days, I designate a staff member to "run the room," and every one of them knows how.

With all of the amps turned on and the PA powered up, there is a warm vibrational hum in this room that makes everything and everyone in it resonate with the same frequency. You can feel it coming up through your feet straight up into your back teeth, and for me, it's like stepping into a river, charged with its own current. It's alive in here. I try to remember who the lead staff member is for the day, shouting over the noise, "Hey, who's in charge around here."

"I think that's you, boss," Eric shouts back, laughing. "Well, OK then. Let's hear what you've been working on." And as the kids find their places, I put a hand on Jake's shoulder and he suddenly remembers the rule about not sitting on the amps, hopping to his feet—which I point at, laughing. He is wearing socks with flip flops, which is not just a bad fashion choice (especially paired with Manitou shorts that are at least two sizes too big for him), but a problem, because for this song he needs to be able to use a foot switch to go to distortion and then off again several times. Jake just stares at me, open-mouthed and blank-eyed. Ethan shakes his head. "We've just decided that I'll kick it on and off for him during the show." I give him a thumbs up. "As long as you've got it. One less thing to worry about." Though, theoretically, I'm in charge now, Steph is clearly running this show. Steph has a resonant alto singing voice and an even deeper and equally resonant speaking voice. More importantly, as an experienced vocalist she has *presence*—a gift she shares with my father—that quality of character that just makes people pay attention to you. At the beginning of the summer I sat the campers down and introduced them to staff, going over the rules I've posted on the door (no noodling, no playing while a staff member is speaking, no taking equipment out of the band room—even your own—without telling a staff member, etc., etc.). I also wanted to get out in front of something else. "As you all know, we have two women on our staff this year. I want to remind you about the last rule on the door, respect each other, the music and yourselves. I know how you guys talk in the cabins and you know how I feel about it. I can't do anything about that.

But in here I make the rules. And when you are in this room you will respect every member of my staff. I will treat sexist language the same way I treat homophobic and racist language—zero tolerance. One shitty comment and you are out—of the band and this room."

Julia has teased me about the speech over beers a few times. Julia, who can silence full grown men with a glance—a side-eye so withering and sharp it's spooky—does not need my protection any more than Steph does. "Don't worry about it. It's just you being a dad. And you're really good at that." It was a nice thing to say—though the compliment carried an unintentional sting. I haven't been feeling like much of a father this summer. Or rather, I've felt as if I've been parenting the wrong children. Once, the band program, like the baseball program, had been a family project in the literal sense. Darius had played keys and even occasionally sung lead in the camper band and had been on staff the previous summer, while also catching for varsity baseball. Before him, my nephew Drew had also been on both "teams"—taking lead vocals and rhythm guitar while starting at catcher.

But Darius never had plans to be here this summer, opting instead to stay home with Rachael and hang out with some of his high school friends. I can hardly blame him. I feel his absence in the room every time I enter it. Almost every one of Darius's camp friends—kids he bonded with over music and baseball, whitewater rafting trips and socials, ghost stories and boat rides, had moved on to other things: internships and music programs at arts camps, or playing with their own bands. We are a victim of our own success. Once a kid falls in love with music, once he realizes he'd rather be in the band room than on a football field, that kid has a hard time justifying a summer at a sports camp. There are just too many other opportunities to play and perform and learn. And this is a lonely place to be without your friends, without your crew, without your family.

"OK," Steph shouts. "Remember the harmony on the second phrase, Max. And Jake. Jake? Jake! Look at me. OK. Concentrate. OK. Look at me. No, not at the floor. At me. Listen. You're supposed to drop out on the bridge—that means stop playing, STOP playing—when Alex is singing by himself—*We can't go on together.* . . ." I stare around in delight, sure that no band in the history of music has ever looked quite like this. Kids, still awkward with being young, carrying baby fat, knobby knees, mouths full of braces. Hair headed in every possible direction, cowlicked and sweaty. What would this album cover look like? Noah hits his sticks together four times. I close my eyes. And listen as Jake comes in, hammering away at a G power chord as if determined to snap his strings. "Caught in a trap. I can't walk out." And then, the surprise, a three-part harmony exploding from the PA, "Because I love you too much baby"—

which has never been on any recording of the song. But should have been. And for the rest of my life will be there. They sound good. Impossibly Good. Seven kids. One brain.

*

In *How the Mind Works*, Steven Pinker infamously refers to music as "auditory cheesecake, an exquisite confection crafted to tickle the sensitive spots of... our mental faculties."[3] My first thought in responding to this is, *so what's wrong with cheesecake? Who doesn't like cheesecake? And who doesn't enjoy having their sensitive spots tickled once in a while.* Though Pinker's statement is irreverent, I suspect that he is mostly right. Like art, the purpose of music seems mostly to engage and stimulate, to trigger and fire certain elements of the neural network. To say this is not to diminish its value; such stimulation and engagement is a large part of why music is part of nearly every ritualistic or celebratory event in human culture. It seems that music, perhaps more than any other art, offers an individual access to the ecstatic, since it ushers us into a place that is both deeply intimate but also shared—that space beside ourselves where we become part of something larger and recognize that connectedness or, as the transcendentalists like to say, that *interconnectedness,* where the differences separating I and thou, now and then, what is human and what is God, break down and dissolve.

And it is music's capacity to facilitate social bonding around that experience that bio and cognitive musicologists like David Huron point to when they theorize that music might have an evolutionary function.[4] Though such a theory is difficult to prove, it seems to hold up well in the face of experience.

To say that music can define cultures, eras, peoples, and individuals is so obvious, so much a given that the statement is almost banal, but in the band room, you can see how this works in real time. The various classifications of popular music: Latin, R&B, Hip-Hop, Country, Christian, Rock, Heavy Metal, Punk, Folk, etc., all speak, not only to style but ethos, not only taste but identity—the rhythms, instrumentation, lyrics, and melodies having embedded in them ways of being, value systems, and codes of behavior that touch on race, ethnicity, gender, sexuality, spirituality, and politics. It can not only be a means of identifying who we are in the world but offer us the ability to reject or resist the world, and the cultural norms that define and confine us. I see this in my own musical tastes and those of my staff and campers. The kid who is into Kendrick Lamar is fundamentally different from the one who shows up in a Pink Floyd t-shirt. Music can cement cultural codes (you can find racism and misogyny throughout the lyrical history of popular music), but it can also be a site of disruption and exploration—regardless of the genre. It not only makes things, it unmakes and remakes them.

From the very beginning of the program, I relished the inherently subversive nature of what we were doing, delighting in how everything we did seemed like one big middle finger to everything I didn't like about boys' summer camps—the toxic masculinity, the herd mentality—while at the same time celebrating so much of what was good about Manitou. At its best, a summer camp can offer kids the first real taste of what it means to be part of something larger than themselves. Every moment is an exercise in team building and an experiment in communal living. And as strange as it may seem to have a program like this, literally in the middle of a sports camp, the process and practice of getting a group of kids to commit to learning and performing music together is a powerful bonding experience that shares many of the values I first learned on the ballfield, playing for my father. In a band room there is no way to ignore how everything you do has an immediate effect on the other people you are playing with. You *have* to listen to each other. You *must* be on the same page. You have to anticipate what the people around you will do (bases, outs, and you). Everyone has to learn to play in the same key, the same rhythm, how to find that "one" together. Each band member has to agree, not only on what songs they will play, what kinds of music they will perform, but to the same *concept* of time and structure and pitch. And they need to learn how to take power and give it back, assuming and giving away the spotlight. A lousy band is not necessarily one without talent, but without trust. It is one that fails to gel—the one where the lead guitarist keeps turning up his amplifier so everyone can hear him even though the rest of the band spent a half an hour doing a sound check before the performance to get the levels right, or who insists on tuning by ear instead of using a tuner, resulting in one guitar being perfectly in tune with itself but out of tune with everything else. The one where the lead singer decides he or she is on *American Idol* and does unplanned (and compositionally pointless) vocal runs, throwing off the harmony, etc.

  For all of that need to accommodate and to blend, there is always something inherently risky, thrilling, and self-exposing about the experience. Nothing, after all, is as frightening or as rewarding as trusting someone else, as allowing yourself to be that vulnerable in a public setting. Academics talk about the classroom being a "safe space"—the intention being to create a learning environment where students can explore ideas and grow without fear. Far too often the result is illusory. And what risks are really being taken when there are so few rules to break and so few consequences? Running an art program in the middle of a boys' sports camp actually feels subversive and if not dangerous, at least absurd. To be different is always to be exposed. When you are on stage, there is no place to hide.

*

I remember this time when your Dad was Director OD. We were all terrified of him back then. But in a kind of "let's all get together and watch a horror movie" kind of terror. Don't get me wrong, there were consequences to pissing off your dad. But we all kind of wanted to experience that moment when he would come storming into the cabin and just lift the roof off the place. You want to poke the bear sometimes. So, we were in our last year and for some reason back then the cabin for the oldest group was right across from your parents' rooms in the lodge. I guess we were being too loud and you couldn't sleep. Or your mom couldn't sleep. You might have already been in a cabin by then. Anyway, your dad kicks the door open and I mean, kicks the door. So when it opens it hits my bunkbed. Like gunshots: bang BANG. He comes walking in like he's Clint Eastwood in High Plains Drifter or something, flicks on the light and just stands there. Everybody's dead quiet. Nobody's moving. I'm sure I was literally holding my breath. I don't remember exactly what Waldo said. Something about it being polite to knock. And your dad just grabs him off the top bunk. Remember, Waldo has never been a small guy, pushing at least a buck 80 even then. And your dad, he just lifts him off the bed and throws him on the floor. Then he just looked at all of us and walked out. We were just laughing all night long. Especially Waldo. Funniest thing ever.

*

Most of my life has been in tension between holding on and letting go. Catch and release. I have lost a child and a spouse. And I have remarried. I lost jobs and left them. And friends. And lovers too. I have moved from state to state. Home to home. Sometimes I think I keep moving so the past can't catch up with me. But there's just no way to travel far enough or fast enough. And I write essays and poems, books of them, about it all. Compulsively turning over the same material. Trying to get it right. Thinking I've done so. And then I write them again, changing the titles, rearranging the words. Maybe this is what it means to be haunted. Not the same thing coming back to you again and again. Not exactly. It comes back, but is always changing, always in disguise. It is *almost*. Almost the thing you remember. Recognizable but strange. Uncanny. And you can't stop staring at it, searching for that part of yourself it offers up. Dreams of heaven and nightmares of hell may be a psychological response to our fear of death. But ghosts are a different matter—they speak to our fear of being forgotten. Of disappearing from this world. Of being erased. And our inability to imagine it going on without us.

There is something inherently uncanny about a summer camp—especially one that has been around for more than half a century. Every boys' and girls' camp in America is a ghost town for ten months of the year—snow piling on the roofs of empty cabins in the winter, grass growing knee-high over ball fields in the spring. Maybe a lone groundskeeper and caretaker roams the property, dog by his side, chasing animals from the offices, bats from empty lofts—alerting the owners if a roof caves in or a pipe bursts. I remember visiting Manitou once in the winter with my family while we were on Christmas break. This was early on in the 10-year hiatus between my first and only year there with Susie and my hobbling return the year of the accident. Darius must have been one or two years old. What I remember most was Cyrus in a bright red snowsuit sitting in a sled with his cousins Drew and Natalie, laughing as I pulled him along the road, through the woods, down to the flagpole area. As a boy I had always thought it would be wonderful to sled down the hill with the cabins forming a corridor on either side and the lake below. But it wasn't. It was alarmingly cold and empty. Without the campers and the staff, without the bugle calls, everything shrouded in white and gray, the place just felt wrong. Off. A breaking of the illusion of permanence, of the world that only existed when we hopped off the bus to laughter and hugs in June and piled back on in August, sunburned and sad.

Too much like the camps across the lake that failed in the early 80s. The ones we'd sometimes visit in the ski-boats in the waning last few days of summer (what we called "the dying times"), when there was little on the schedule other than packing and cleaning and the unit leaders had to be inventive in finding ways to entertain the kids and keep them out of the cabins and off the courts as they piled up with trunks and duffle bags. I remember walking around the grounds of Camp Lakeridge fifteen years after it had closed its gates forever. Everything about the place was eerie. I remember the cabins that had caved in from too many seasons untended. I remember the rust-red flakes of paint floating on stalks of uncut grass. Piles of docks stacked beside the waterfront, waiting for a summer that never came. Beneath what appeared to be the camp dining hall, we found a large wooden plaque in the shape of a doghouse, Snoopy dancing on the roof. Stenciled in black cursive, "You're a Good Man, Charlie Brown." I was 12 years old and felt as if I'd just walked across my own grave. All thing pass, for certain. But they also repeat, time looping back over itself.

 But summer camps are a place of ghost stories told at night, flashlights pressed beneath the acned and peach-fuzzed chin of the storyteller. Every former camper and counselor knows a variation on a chilling tale of wild-men and hermits creeping out of the woods to steal children or cut off an errant arm hanging below a mattress, of boys being pulled down into the darkness of a murky lake during swim period. It doesn't matter that few camps could survive the actual death of a camper—the world being the litigious place it is—every camp has a story "the directors don't want you to know about." About the curse of Old Bunk 7, its ruins rotting in the woods behind Bunk 6, the ghosts of its campers still trapped within, or Bunk 13 sunk into the ground during a rainstorm, boys trapped eternally in the mud, or the haunted piano in the theater that plays in early hours of the morning all on its own, its keys pressed by the ghostly fingers of a theater director's daughter who, fifty years ago, had fallen one summer from a catwalk to the concrete floor 20 feet below. All of it is nonsense, of course. Old Bunk 7 does sit back there, pushed among the pines to rot after a winter storm caved its roof, but its only occupants are raccoons. There never was a Bunk 13 (why tempt fate?). And the theater building, though ominous when empty, at night, was built in the early 90s and nearly all of our theater directors have been bachelors, and bachelorettes. Most of them gay and childless. They did catch a hermit—a man who lived off the grid, in the woods, in tents and lean-to's, stealing what he needed from local backyards and sheds. That news set off a storm among ex-campers on Facebook. But he never hurt anyone. And as far as we can tell, he never came to Manitou—at least not in the summer.

 To return to a place for two months of every year is to constantly be reminded of the past while facing absences and change, ones that accumulate too fast to manage, and remind us of how blindingly fast our lives move. It's like watching people dance beneath a strobe light. Everything leaping across the gaps—too fast for the brain to process. Constantly catching up and trying to make sense of the darkness and how these images connect to each other. Life as a flipbook. For a long time coming back to Manitou was stabilizing—a way to connect the threads of life. But then the threads began to snap. Andy Arenson used to say, "it's a tough place to grow old." And it's true. Even the most popular summer camps struggle to retain good staff year after year. Very few people have jobs that allow them to take the summers off, which is why our staff is made up mostly of people who are in education, are incapable of holding down regular jobs, are in that brief liminal moment between college and entering the workforce, or who live non-traditional lifestyles—wanderers who equate rootlessness with freedom. The result is a staff that is diverse in age and culture and constantly renewing itself. It also might explain the almost religious and cult-like devotion to ritual, to the past, and to story that permeates the place. When the cast of characters keeps changing, the setting, the pattern, the rhythm must repeat. There has to be something we can rely on. There must be stories—myths and legends—if only to hold the pieces together. To give them purpose and meaning.

For the first several years of the program I struggled to have consistency on staff. Asking professional or even part-time musicians and entertainers to give up entire summers to work at a boys' summer camp is to ask them to give up other, more lucrative, opportunities to play and perform. Very few bands will wait for their bassist or drummer while they are off coaching kickball games. And this is not just true of the musicians, but every area of camp. When we return, half of our staff boast about it as an accomplishment. I tell my staff that my job at Manitou might begin in June, but I'm working on it from January on, contacting older staff—seeing who is coming back, who isn't, and recruiting new people to fill the inevitable holes. In ten years of running a program I have had over twenty-five different instructors on staff, replacing two to three a year. I struggle every year to make peace with the absence of those who do not return, telling them and myself that moving on is healthy and that what you want for your friends is for their lives to progress, to change and develop. People who *do* continually return year after year, even those who have the summers free, often seem to struggle to make progress in their lives. Marriages fail. Jobs are lost. People develop addictions and dependencies. And recently the losses have become grimmer. I've gotten to know and love and say goodbye to so many, too many people to count.

I've been thinking a lot about losses this summer. Because that's what you do as you get old. As the world moves forward around you and like a heavy stone in a river, you stop moving with it. It becomes harder and harder to relate to younger staff and you feel more ridiculous trying to. And after a while, you get the sensation of walking over graves and through ghosts. Real and imagined. My third summer running the program, I tried to have the new staff over for drinks. It didn't go well. The conversation was stilted. It was awkward.

In the beginning, Rachael loved hosting the band, Tristan, Davis, and John, for drinks and conversation. We'd stay up playing and listening to music, laughing and talking until Rachael or John passed out on the couch. Or Rachael went to bed. Sometimes we'd keep things going even then. Rach would climb into bed and we'd just wish her goodnight, turning the volume on the record player down a bit so she could sleep. But that summer I had an even younger staff and those get togethers just felt strange. "Joel," she said, "Davis and John aren't walking through that door." And though things actually got better in the years that followed—especially after Andy Ambat came over from India and then brought his brother Reuben and his friend, DT, creating a strong stable core to the program, I could already feel the clock ticking down. I think I spent a good ten years waiting for Davis and John to walk through the door, and half-thinking they might—looking for shades of them in new faces, in the thump of the bass or the bending string of a guitar.

For a while the losses were of that nature, people moving on with their lives, doing other things with them—getting jobs, getting married, having children, pursuing careers. I could still call Davis or John up when I needed them, follow their bands on twitter and Facebook. But I could feel myself becoming part of their past. A face in the rearview. And then the losses became more literal. Andy Arenson was the canary in the coal mine.

Andy was one of the first people to call me when I was recovering at King's hospital in Amman, Jordan. I didn't even know I had a phone in the room until it rang. And I couldn't believe it when I heard his voice on the line. My father handed the phone to me in disbelief. I had no idea how he got the number. The day after Andy called, I had to ask my father if it really happened. Or if it was just some dream within the dream I was floating in and out of again—a voice from the past in a moment when I desperately needed to hear just that. I don't know how many days after the accident it was. I was on heavy doses of morphine entering my veins from a bag suspended over my head. Wires were strung taut to pins set on either side of my right knee. Bone fragments had crushed my sciatic nerve, causing an intense burning and stabbing sensation that ran up the back of my leg periodically but without any pattern or rhythm. I remember I had this button that I could push when I was in pain, releasing the morphine in long cylindrical drops that would travel down the tube and into my veins. I was doing a lot of floating.

I told him that I was coming back to camp (it never occurred to me that there wasn't a place waiting there for me) and that I wanted him to be there too. "It would mean a lot to me. I need to come home." The truth was, I really didn't have much choice. I couldn't take care of my son without help and that meant living with my mother and father for a while. And my convalescing in their home would mean they needed their summer salaries more than ever. Still, my plan to bring our surviving son, Darius, back to a place that Susie had hated intensely the one summer we worked there together was almost an affront to her memory.

I don't talk about that summer with Susan very often. Trying to work there with her in 1993 was a terrible idea. Camp is hard on even the strongest relationships. And ours was always marked by volatility. Susie was brilliant and beautiful, not yet the literary star she would become in just a few years but already finding herself as an artist—writing poetry about her family in Iran, taking incredible black and white photographs, and carving dark, vibrant oil paintings onto canvases, forgoing the brush for the palette knife. But we were both intense, both artists trying make space for ourselves in the world while trying to figure out how to be a part of each other's lives. And we came from drastically different worlds. My father liked to joke that I "married up," and I did. My family was hanging by the last rung to middle class in a wealthy town. Susie grew up in an apartment with marble floors overlooking Mont Blanc. Cabin life was not for her. I remember that it rained the first night we were there, and she woke to a steady drip of water landing on her forehead as well as a puddle forming inside the suitcase she had yet to unpack. Things went downhill from there. It took ten years and an accident that cost the lives of half my family to return to Manitou. But from the bed of King's hospital, making that choice seemed as natural as breathing.

*

By the summer of 2013 I had been watching Andy fall apart for nearly a decade. Looking back on it, I realize he was bipolar. And that he had been for as long as I'd known him. Our cabins were on opposite sides of the property. Mine, up by the dining hall. His, down by the lake. But over so many summers we had developed a morning routine, meeting at the middle when he'd walk up the hill to have a cigarette in the counselor parking lot before breakfast as I worked on my first cup of coffee. And we'd talk. Andy was one of the only Manitou directors who remembered Susie from her one summer working there and who would sometimes talk to me about her and about the accident, about my life before my return to camp. At times, just asking me outright, what I remembered (awakening on the side of desert highway), what I dreamed about (shards of glass exploding outward, a body thrown into the darkness). He was also one of the few directors who supported and enjoyed my music program, never missing a show. "You've created something new here. You don't know how hard that is to do. How rare." What is a little strange is that when I was a camper, I didn't worship Andy the way that my friends did. He seemed unhinged to me. Unstable. Unsteady. Someone to stay away from. But I think in some ways we both carried a darkness, and we were both using this place to push it down and away. There was a pattern to Andy's summers, starting out every June with a burst of energy and enthusiasm and then gradually growing more disengaged, then despondent, before ending the summer with two weeks of not showing up for meetings, skipping meals, threatening to leave, and promising not to come back. Like my father, Andy was a legend—if one with a more turbulent history—and like my father, that was part of the problem. In his mid-twenties and into his thirties Andy had grown from an obscure and eccentric archery instructor to the head of a lacrosse program that rivaled my father's baseball program in prestige and quality. He was also a character who seemed to step right out of *Meatballs* or *Wet Hot American Summer*. Sporting a mass of curly brown hair and a bushy moustache, he always seemed poised on the edge of madness—sometimes dangerously so. Whenever the camp needed to throw an activity together at the last minute, Andy was the man called on to fill the gap in the evening activity schedule, organizing "special events" like Steve Hirsch night—during which campers would chug milkshakes stirred up in garbage cans with lacrosse sticks and wiffle ball bats, then spin in circles until they threw up in the outfield of diamond #1, or Snipe Hunt—an evening activity that required counselors, who were each assigned a random number of points (or bounty) to hide in the woods lining the camp. They would then shout "snipe" until campers discovered then chased them across the darkening fields in screaming packs, the pursuit ending in a pile of bodies and shouts of "my-man-one-two three." Andy's events were absurd and carnivalesque, torn equally from the pages of *Lord of the Flies* and *Where the Wild Things Are*. They also tended to result in a full infirmary and a day of angry phone calls from parents.

    Of course, the campers adored him.

    But his dark side could be frightening too. He was asked to leave camp in the 80s after increasingly erratic behavior that included threatening another director. Apparently, the man had returned from an out night in Waterville to find Andy sitting on the hallway floor across from his room, mumbling to himself as he repeatedly threw a bowie knife into his door. That's the story anyway. I have no idea if it is true or not. So many of the stories we tell here are apocryphal, less true than representative. And Andy's camp persona could make it easy to forget that he had another life away from this place where he was a beloved and award-winning educator in the Baltimore school system. And even easier to forget that, beneath the manic, gleeful energy, there was a person in there who was struggling—a lonely man who never had children of his own and who had fallen in love and married a single mother only to see her succumb to disabling and violent schizophrenia. In the last few years, I knew him, he was caring for his ex-wife in his home as she died of cancer.

    After that there were other losses. Bob Bulloch, our long-time waterfront director, died of brain cancer. And then there was Chase Adkins—a beautiful young guitarist I had recruited from the English program at Marshall University where I teach American Literature and Creative Writing. Chase was loose-limbed and long. He'd glide through the halls of the English building, arms swinging as if to his own internal rhythm. He was also brilliant—a talented scholar, writer and musician who could compose in any genre. In classes, he would sit in silence for most of the period, listening attentively but only speaking when spoken to and then very carefully, as if each word had to be considered, placed in the right spot, and then given a chance to settle before the next one could come. But when he did speak, people listened. It wasn't too hard to see myself in Chase's blond hair and blue eyes—and he had a voice that was eerily similar to my own.

    There is a magic to harmony—when you find someone you can sing with, whose voice is complementary to your own, it's like discovering a part of yourself that's been walking around without you, outside of you. An empty space suddenly fills. I had enjoyed having Chase in my classroom, instinctively liking him. But I *loved* singing with Chase. The first time he showed up in the band room, he blew us away with his guitar skills, but it was when we covered "I Feel Fine" by the Beatles that something special happened, our voices locking into place immediately. At the time, Julia was on the photography staff, but I was stealing her away whenever possible to play drums for us. I remember finishing the song, the last phrase ringing through the room. Then the stunned silence that followed. I knew right away that we had something special.

Though I saw myself, and even heard myself, in Chase, there were important differences. He had no interest in athletics, for example, and was not much of a talker. His energy was different too. I am restless and intense. Slower to anger than my father but just as sensitive to insult and just as explosive when triggered. Chase had the ability to calm me down. To just look me in the eyes and say, "everything is going to be fine" and get me to believe it. Chase was, from the beginning, a strange fit for Manitou. People liked him, but they were never sure of what to do with him. Like me, he struggled to buy into the place—finding too many of the activities absurd. He was also—like many of my musicians— hopelessly addicted to cigarettes at a place where cigarettes were forbidden. He couldn't even get through a couple of hours without a puff. So I would schedule "coffee breaks" in the middle of practices and laugh as he ran across the ball field to the nearest parking lot where he could get his nicotine fix, then turn around, run the one-hundred yards back to the band room (in sandals and jeans) sweating and out of breath so he could finish the instructional.

My whole family loved Chase. Even Darius, who often struggled with how I seemed to always be collecting proxy sons and daughters, treating my staff and students like adopted children. Sometimes I wonder if all these years, I've simply been trying to replace Cyrus—if Manitou offered too easy an opportunity to fill the massive space in my life left by his death. Chase didn't quite make it through the summer, leaving two weeks before the end of camp to see his grandfather who had just been diagnosed with pancreatic cancer.

Two months after that, Chase was gone. Asphyxiating on the floor of his apartment above his father's garage—a hypodermic needle six inches from his hand.

*

     As a writer of poetry and creative nonfiction, I am hyperconscious of the power of two words "I remember"—an assertion of identity nearly as powerful as "I am," and in some ways more so, largely because it is selective. The listener, the reader, knows that what is to come is important because it has been retained, kept safe in the storage shed of memory, and because it warrants retelling—at least to the author. To write down the memory, to record it, or to pass it on, is a gift of the self. It is to take an heirloom out of a box, saying "this is of me, from me. Here." Who we are is constructed out of such stuff. I know the stories of my father will tell me more about the person reciting them than they ever would of him. The man in those stories is the one they need him to be. Every photograph is really a portrait of the one who holds the camera.

     But what do I make of the fact that so much of my life and my son's life—who we are—has been defined by an event that neither of us has a clear memory of. Darius was only three years old, and I was asleep in the back seat when our van drove into the sand truck parked across Kings Highway somewhere between Amman and Aqaba. I was knocked unconscious. I did not see my oldest son thrown through the windshield. I did not witness the emergency crew arrive to pull me from the wreck. I did not ride with my mother-in-law in the helicopter with Susie. Or watch as the light passed from her eyes. I did not hear the sound of Darius crying—his leg broken, his brother and mother gone, his grandmother rising above and away from him as he was trundled into an ambulance. I did not hear the helicopter blades buffet the air around us all. Sometimes I have an image of the stars over the Dead Sea. Sometimes I think I remember searing pain and the road beneath my back. But are these even memories? Most of what I know, I know from the stories I have been told of the accident. Most of what I see is what I imagine. Perhaps it is not the memory of an event that shapes us but its effects—a person being one star in a constellation, subject to the push and pull—the forces of everything in its galaxy. Its identity a product of relationships.

*

So back then your father was basically running the place. He was the baddest guy on the mountain, know what I mean? Anyway, they had to fire someone. I don't remember the reason. I don't even think he was on your dad's radar. But I guess the guy was a little volatile so of course they called your dad in to give him the news. Guy didn't take it well. I could hear them—the guy shouting, your dad staying calm but stern, the whole time he was packing his stuff up and headed to his car. He was by the picnic area, about a hundred yards up the hill and on his way out before he shouts—"you have a son and I know where he sleeps."

Well, about five of us spent the next few nights sitting in the back of the office watching the road that leads down to the lodge. We got these guns from riflery. And I remember your dad sitting up all night on the steps in the dark, the porchlight on him, mosquitoes flying around his head, that rifle across his thighs. Waiting. Watching.

*

    People do not tell stories of my mother or my sisters at camp. And that is a blessing to all of us. Stories of women at Manitou are rarely if ever flattering. The tales that do get told serve the frustrated masculine fantasies of campers and counselors who have spent eight weeks in a concentrated testosterone factory. Stories of hypersexual nurses visiting CITs on the ball fields or in the woods. Stories of directors' daughters slipping off to cabin porches or docks for an illicit assignation. Stories of Matoaka staff showing up at bonfires and wandering off into the woods with multiple partners. Little to none of it is based in truth. And none of it is worth repeating. Until recently there were few "roles" available to women here, both in terms of position and identity. Nowhere is the mother/whore dynamic more rigid than a boys' camp. And though my mother might have seemed a perfect fit for "camp mom," it wasn't really a title that suited her. Elegantly beautiful, blond, blue-eyed, and chatty, my mother could seem a little flighty, even silly, at times, falling into stereotypical gender tropes. But that bright veneer masks an underlying toughness and intelligence. My father and I might be the ones with advanced degrees in literature, my sister Tina might have an Ivy-league education, and Lisa—the child most similar to my father—might be the talented therapist, but my mother is the best-read member of the family and may be the most talented, creatively. She could hold her own as an athlete as well, the two qualities combining to form a gifted ballet dancer who built a respected dance and gymnastic business in our hometown of Sharon, where she is loved and remembered fondly by generations of women who attended her class in the Community Center overlooking Lake Massapoag. Initially arriving as the very-pregnant wife to the new athletic director, my mother quickly found her role at Manitou, using her years of experience waterskiing as a camper and counselor at Camp Nakomis as the foundation to build one of the strongest ski programs in camping. There was a time when my mother and father were not only the most competent directors at camp, they were the best teachers, too, capable of demonstrating to campers the skills that they were instructing, and even a few too difficult or dangerous to teach. Well into her mid-sixties, my mother could both amaze and worry her entire staff by insisting on reminding them of what she could do—hopping off the ski boat into the chilly waters of East Pond and grabbing the rope as it curled behind her in the glassy dark surface before shouting "hit it" to an anxious, if smiling, boat driver and exploding up and out in a curtain of spray. Her routine was graceful and fluid and I've watched it since I was a shivering little boy, wrapped in towel as the wind whipped my hair in front of me. Watching my mother as she'd reach down casually like she was slipping off a sandal to remove one ski and tuck it under her arm while inserting one fragile ankle into the triangle of the ski rope, switching to a heel-hold while raising the ski above her head. It was jaw-dropping theater. Executed with a pointed toe and a brilliant, defiant grin.

And without getting her hair wet.

And whenever I fool myself into mistaking my mother's hummingbird-wing disposition as weakness, I remember that image of her, arms upraised, the wake unraveling behind her in a long white ribbon.

My father may have been king of the ball fields, but for a good twenty-five years, my mother ruled East Pond. And though now there are women in charge of programs and units throughout camp, she was the first woman to have a position of any significance at Manitou. And campers adored her. It was a memorable moment in every camper's life when my mother would get up after the evening meal to announce that Neil Feldman, Andy Lampert, Mark Lipman, "got up on skis today and went all the way around the lake." And though it might have caused a little ribbing for an older camper, having my mother hand you that little felt achievement patch was a rite of passage for all of us. And the cheers that filled the dining hall were genuine.

Those days are gone. The last decade has seen my mother suffer multiple knee injuries, bouts of skin cancer, and even a mini stroke. It's been years since she's even gotten into the water with a camper, never mind ski and instruct from the boat when she instructs at all. And the skills she grew up with—slalom, trick skiing—have given way to wake boarding and wake surfing in popularity. She can't spend as much time under the sun and like my father, has less and less control over a program she once coordinated and ran. Ironically, it was a handful of women who began pushing my mother aside—twenty-somethings who looked at her and saw Martha Stewart when she was really much closer in spirit to Martha Graham. I can feel it happening to me even in my little program.

As much as my mother has been obscured by my father's legend here, she built a space for herself, and leaving this place will be hard on her. On this hill, on that lake, she had her own friends and a chance to be not just a mother or a wife, but a person. For eight weeks a year, she had her own job and other people to watch the kids. Even when she ran the dance program in Sharon, she had to include her children in the classes and have half an eye tilted in their direction regardless of what she was teaching. She had to worry about getting home in time to get dinner on the table and rise early enough to pack lunches and complete the laundry before dropping a needle on the record player and choreographing routines for her afternoon classes. There was no time for herself. Every day was scheduled to the minute—and every minute was devoted to someone else. But at Manitou, her children were relatively safe and free to roam the camp with one hundred other adults to watch them. Meals were someone else's problems. And that meant she was free as well. For a woman who got married at nineteen and had her first child at twenty, that must have been liberating.

Now, when my father leaves the table at a meal or storms away, she will wipe at her eyes and tell me, "I know what the rest of my life will look like. It will be about him—about taking care of him. And that's ok. That's what I signed up for." Then she'll shake her head and pat my hand, laughing, "But we're not there yet."

We are close, though.

*

    The afternoon period at camp is devoted to an intracamp activity known as College League. And I use the word "devoted" in its root sense. Almost any former camper from any American boys' or girls' camp is familiar with the concept of Color War, a camping tradition in which campers are split into two teams represented by colors that will then compete in a series of games. Though Manitou has its own Color War between the teams of Maroon and Gray— a four-day event, occurring at the beginning of August and finishing off our program—the rest of the summer is dominated by College League, in which the camp is split into four teams, each representing a college and lead by a "dean." This tradition, unique in camping, has become a signature part of our program. It's also the one period of the day when I have to make a conscious shift from creative to athletic staff, usually serving as umpire for a softball game or a line judge for flag football. I prefer softball because an efficient umpire can keep a game moving pretty quickly.

    When my father isn't in a rage during a morning meeting, or coaching baseball, he motors around the camp by himself in his golf cart with nowhere to go and nothing really to do. My father has never drifted through a day in his life. He is purpose-driven and always has a plan and a destination. So when I walk across the track in the early afternoon and see him sitting on a cart in the middle of an empty soccer field, watching a flag football game from a distance, the image hits me like a blow to the stomach. He is fuming. And when I jog over and hop up into the passenger seat of the cart, he launches into a diatribe—"no one told me we were pushing back the softball games a half an hour. We're all out there on the field, ready to play and that idiot Waldo comes running over to tell me that I have to wait. I told him to get the hell out of my park. He just smiled that idiot grin of his and walked over to the coaches. Next thing I know everybody is leaving. So I'm sitting here looking at my watch doing nothing. All because of him." The truth is that somebody did tell him about the time change. I know this because I was that somebody. And in fact I had told him repeatedly and been asked by Waldo to remind him, and so reminded him during lunch. Several times. I feel a bit guilty about the situation because I hold some responsibility for it. Softball games tend to run shorter than the other sports, especially the six-inning games played by our youngest campers and on one occasion, having been given a period off, I found multiple children under the age of 10 wandering around in the woods as I jogged through the path along the ropes course. Some of them weren't even on camp property—all of them looked as if they had rolled around in a mud puddle. Eyes on the ground, kicking at rocks and sticks, they told me that their games were over and it was hot on the ball fields, so they were hunting frogs and salamanders for the upcoming scavenger hunt. After herding them back to their teams and coaches I found Dave Schiff to let him know what happened. This was his solution: start the games for the younger kids a little bit later. Let them watch the older kids play football for a bit before they got bored, while they were still anticipating their games and had a place to be. Unfortunately for my father, this meant another change in his routine. And seven full days into the adjustment, he is still forgetting about it. My reminding him only seems to make him angrier and more confused. I've given up on telling him that we'd had this same discussion yesterday and the day before that. Instead, I sit and I listen, as if for the first time, nodding my head, trying to direct his attention to something, anything else. But my father has come to suspect even my presence. "So what are you doing here?" he asks. And he's right to be suspicious. My father's memory lapses have not gone unnoticed by the coaches or the athletes of the games he is officiating. And even though his mistakes are rare (he keeps track of the score on a notepad and uses a mechanical "indicator" to keep track of balls, strikes, and outs), those few errors have eroded the trust they have in his abilities. There are also safety concerns. You umpire softball from behind the mound and a few days ago he was hit in the head by a hard line drive—a comebacker hammered right back through the infield. "He went down like a sack of bricks," a breathless junior counselor told me, "but he just gets right back up, waves us all off the field, and finishes the game. Like nothing happened. The whole time he's wiping blood off his forehead with a handkerchief. I mean, it was incredible." After that, Dave talked to me about asking my dad if he would wear a batting helmet on the field. I just laughed, "A batting helmet. I can't even get him to wear sunblock." But I did promise to watch his games from then on, sitting in the dugout, keeping track of the count, the inning, the number of outs.

*

When most people think of themselves as "persons" they imagine a continuous line of development—an unbroken sequence, in which who they "are" began at one point in the past and evolved gradually, through time, with each experience contributing to the creation of the person they have become. So the person they once were is *essentially* the same person they are now, just one who has grown and developed. This is why so many people perceive their lives as "journeys," what Galen Strawson calls a "diachronic self."[5] But I do not see myself as being on a journey of any kind. The lines are broken and tangled into knots, threads frayed at the ends. When I say that upon hearing a song, I am "once again" the boy running through the office, chased by his babysitter, or the boy at Friday night services, praying that he will be selected for an achievement badge in *something, anything*, or one of three children sitting on a bed with Uncle Bobbie in a building that no longer exists, its roof having finally given in to a century of rain and snow, or the exhausted young man, rocking back and forth, singing John Lennon's "Beautiful Boy (Darling Boy)" to a child who seven years into the future will fly through a windshield on a desert highway somewhere between Amman and Aqaba, I am admitting that I am now, fundamentally, not that boy or that man.

This is both frightening and freeing.

And maybe, also, a bit easier on the heart. If I am not that man, then I am not responsible for the things that man did, the choices he made—like letting his oldest son travel in the front seat of a van, unbelted, that night in the desert so many years ago. And my life does not have to be conditioned or defined by the trauma and terror he experienced. Even if I do remember what it was like to be in that head, that body, those moments, the memories can feel strangely distanced—as if I'm less remembering than listening to someone read a story to me about a character in a novel. I even wonder, at times, if the brain injury I suffered during the accident didn't shake something loose in me, breaking some synapse, erasing some fundamental connection. And sometimes I feel that way—as if my ten-year marriage to Susan was some dream of a life in one of those stories my students turn in, ending anticlimactically with the words "and then I woke up."

Is this why I write so often in the present tense, creating a false "now" for the reader, taking forays into the past, sorties, stepping quietly through the jungle of memory, anxious of ambush, the whole time praying for a safe return? Is this why I wrote my first collection of essays about the accident as if in a race? As if my hold on the years and days and minutes leading up to that moment was slipping, my fingers slick and grasping a greased rope? Is this why I can recall the sound of Cyrus's voice only through my own descriptions of it?

Or maybe the blurring of those times is a matter of a different kind of survivalism—self-defense. Defense of the self I believe I am in spite of, *in defiance of*, the evidence of memory—of what I've done. Of who I've been and what has happened to me. If "he" failed as a father, I will be everyone's father. If "he" failed to protect them, I will protect everyone.

Or go crazy trying.

A year after the accident, a friend of mine told me that I really did seem like a different man. For better or worse. "Wayne just hates you now. You know what he told me? He said, 'The Joel I knew died in the accident.'" My reaction to that was a reflexive, and surprising, "Good. I hope he did." Of course, Wayne was Rachael's boyfriend before we got together. So he had his reasons.

I suspect that the personality changes I experienced after the accident were also an act of will, a conscious choice to allow myself to let go of myself and become someone new—no matter who that hurt. Sometimes I wonder if my father is worthy of at least that much generosity. If we can forgive him for what he does in the middle of the night while in the grips of a dream—if my mother can pretend it didn't happen even as the bruises appear on her arms—can we forgive him for other things he can't even remember having done? Can we grant him absolution, the freedom to not have to be the man that people remember? Who should be a memory? Who should have to be?

We all say that my father struggles to let go. And to some extent that is true. He holds on to the things and people he loves with both hands. Which is why he had to be forced into retirement from high school coaching years after it became apparent that he was struggling to remember who his players were. And it is why he can't stop returning to Manitou—even after the owners cut his salary in half. Even after they bulldozed the cabin he'd been living in and moved him to a smaller place right next to the outdoor basketball court.

*

"They said I could come back and live in that cabin as long as I wanted," he says, launching a finger like a dart across the flagpole area to the green lot where his summer home used to be. Where now a very large brown building blocks out the view of the lake, a two-story structure that attempts to be half-cabin, half-New England Colonial. I have come over on what has become a nightly ritual. Walking down to their cabin as the last mournful notes of Taps play across the camp and the lights in Sophomore Village have begun to flicker off to the sound of counselors ordering children into bed. Sometimes I drag an off-duty staff member along with me, either grabbing them on my way down the hill or giving them a heads up at dinner to meet me there. Sometimes I bring the whole crew and a guitar. My dad loves my program and my staff and takes great pleasure in playing host—mixing drinks and telling stories. And he has always had a soft spot for any kind of artist, especially musicians. I often wonder if my father would have been a singer or an actor if he was born in a different place to different people—ones with more resources or more exposure to culture.

  I even spent a summer or two trying to teach my father to play. After my staff and I had performed a shambolic but energetic set at a local bar, he mentioned that he would love to get up there with us and play a song someday. I thought it was a great idea ("I can teach anyone to play three chords," I told my staff, "We could play 'Folsom Prison Blues' or maybe something by Elvis—'Hound Dog' or 'Mystery Train,' maybe"). My mother loved the idea as well, hoping that learning an instrument might help him with his memory. So she bought him a guitar, an Ovation Celebrity with a pure, almost haunting tone, and we got to work. I tried every technique I knew to get him to remember the chord shapes, the names of the strings, the progressions. But it didn't take. Every time I worked with him, it was like it was the first time he'd ever picked up the instrument. It was frustrating and frightening. My father is physically and mentally gifted. And has always been capable of picking almost anything up, seemingly without effort. My mother was almost angered by how quickly he picked up waterskiing, for example, going from beginner to expert in a matter of days.

  At the time, I told myself that that was the problem. He'd never really had to work at anything this hard. He was used to things just coming to him. And so he expected this to be the same. I got on him about not practicing enough—"it needs to become body memory. Just feel the shapes your fingers make on the strings. No. Don't look at the chart. You have to go by touch. If you practice enough, you'll get it." And I worked to keep the frustration out of my voice, sounding far too much like he once did when he couldn't teach me how to throw a curveball or shorten my swing. "I know you can do this. Come on now. Concentrate." What I couldn't face was that this wasn't a matter of character or work ethic. He wasn't not practicing because he was lazy, but because he was frustrated and ashamed. No matter how hard he tried he couldn't retain the information long enough to embody it, even if he picked the guitar back up an hour after the lesson. He just couldn't remember.

Now I keep the guitar up in the band room and occasionally pick it up when I'm in a mournful place—which has been too often this summer.

Tonight it is just me, no staff. And in the ten minutes I have been there, my father has already poked his head out of his cabin twice to shout at campers who insist on shooting baskets, even though the lights are off, even though they could go up to Alumni Hall and play there. The older kids can roam the camp until almost midnight. And if they come across a ball that has not been locked up, having rolled under a bleacher or into the bushes, they simply can't resist the temptation of launching it through the darkness in the general direction of the hoop. Which is right in front of my parents' front porch. The result is an inevitable roof-rattling "thump" that shakes the entire building.

I sip my father's cocktail of choice—a sweet and insanely strong Southern Comfort Manhattan, dry with a twist, the Sox game droning deep into extra innings. "God, I miss the sunsets on the back porch. Remember that? Shows you what their promises are worth." I do remember it. I remember JD making that promise one evening over drinks, slapping my father on the shoulder as he said it, and I remember, even then, feeling uncomfortable about it. I knew my father was incapable of a graceful exit. It's not in his nature.

It is also a strange side-effect of his dementia that my father can't remember if he's eaten breakfast or taken a shower on any given day but will fixate on something said to him five years ago and repeat it like a prayer. "As long as I wanted to keep coming back." And I understand his anger—not so much because JD and Schiff reneged on a "promise," but because they ever made that promise. In my family, we treat every statement of intent like a covenant. "I will" is a blood pact and "I'll try" means "unless I die trying." We do what we say we are going to do and expect others to do the same. This is a matter of integrity and principle, and when someone doesn't keep their word—we read it not only as a betrayal but an indictment of that person's character.

But that's the problem with promises. Circumstances change. The world changes. And we change with it. We have to or we don't just get left behind, we find ourselves staring into an increasingly distant past, trying to hold it together as it slips away. Back when this little cabin we are having drinks in was plenty big enough for Dave Schiff. Back when no one could foresee him ever getting married, never mind having two kids. Back when it seemed equally unimaginable that my father would become increasingly forgetful to the point where he was incapable of completing most of the tasks he had performed so easily and effectively for so many years as Athletic Director, they made a promise. But the promise they made was to *that* Joel Peckham. And though my father is still that man, he no longer is that *person*.

So I nod my head in sympathy, even as I tell him, "But this place is perfect for you now. You don't need the extra rooms. The living room is larger. It's so much easier to entertain people." The truth is, it bothers me too, and not because of the basketballs. I feel the absence of that place even more than when our first camp home, the lodge, fell to time and weather. It would have been one thing to simply move my mother and father out. To say, "we need the space and it's just the two of you." If they had moved in with their kids and lived there, I could have dealt with that. But they had to bulldoze it. Erase it. Build on top of it. I thought I was ok with that until I came to camp and found it gone.

I've often said that you can return to a place but not a time. But places change too. I remember that cabin. Vividly. Even before my parents moved there, when it was still just a three-room split-log box on stilts with a tiny gray porch and a bright yellow door, it was one of the places in camp I felt most welcome. I spent eight summers of my life scurrying around the camp with my sisters, babysitters, and nannies chasing me out of the woods and off the docks, before I was old enough to be in a cabin and really participate in most camp activities. With my mother running the ski program and my father running almost everything else, I was on my own with my sisters quite a bit. My parents had to rely on other sets of eyes and hands to keep us safe, to report back to them anything we did wrong. And for the most part we were safe, surrounded by people who cared for us. Who loved us and protected us.

Camp was a good place for a little boy to be—a place where I had hundreds of older brothers and opportunities to explore any activity I wanted. A place where I could be certain that everyone around me was looking out for me. And one of the places I could always go was up the steps and onto the porch of what was, then, Aunt Sue's cabin—where hard candies waited for me in a wooden bowl. "Just one," she'd say, and I'd grab two, running off again as she laughed in my wake. By the time Bobby had bought the camp and my parents moved into the place, I was already a camper and Lisa and Tina had moved on to Matoaka, our sister camp across the lake. So the little cabin was plenty of room for them. But as the family grew, the cabin grew with it: a master bedroom was built onto the back, and the original bedrooms used as guest rooms for visits of children and grandchildren. Slowly the cabin stretched back across the lawn, long and low, with a back porch finally added in the early 2000s. There my parents would entertain family and friends, my dad mixing and drinking Cosmos and Manhattans while the sun disappeared over the lake.

Maybe it is not my father who is unwilling to let go of things. Maybe it is the people around him. Maybe we are all trying hold him to account. To be who we need him to be so we can continue to live in the world as we remember it—to thank him, to punish him, to forgive him, to remind us of who we were and are. Maybe to lose him is to lose a sense of who we are. How could this not be true for me? I am Joel Peckham, *Jr.*, after all. Juniah. Jo Jo. JPJ.

There is something about this place that makes it hard to grow and change the way that people must. The longer you stay in a place, the more you become defined by it or become a defining aspect of it. You stop being a person and become a character. And a character isn't an identity, not really. "To have character," Amélie O. Rorty writes in *The Identities of Persons*, "is to have reliable qualities, to hold tightly to them through temptations to swerve and change. A person of character is neither bribed nor corrupted; he stands fast, is steadfast. . . . Characters are dear to us because they are predictable."[6] Even to have character is to suggest a stability and integrity that is part performance, part imposition based on the expectations and needs of an audience—or what the actor imagines those expectations to be. Our lives change quickly, and we reach for stable things. Returning campers getting off the buses after ten months away from the place search the crowd of staff members for familiar faces, and they run to them. Often leaping into embraces.

I both loved and hated the fact that I was a fundamentally different person at Manitou. Not a professor of English. Not a writer. Not even a widower. I was JPJ, band director. And I both embraced and resented the absurdity of that. Was liberated by it. But also trapped in it. Every year I would spend ten months in a profession where I was regarded with an almost humorless seriousness, where I was a semi-tragic figure, Hamlet in the graveyard no matter what class I was teaching or meeting I was in. Then I would arrive at camp and all of that would disappear. Suddenly, no one took me seriously. And asking to be taken seriously in such a setting only makes one more ridiculous. Even once the music program had developed into a one of the more established parts of Manitou's culture, it was never exactly popular or cool to the people who decided what was cool here. Once, after a particularly good performance, my lead guitarist, Andy Ambat, made a point to tease Waldo about it. "I guess we're not so much of a joke anymore, huh?" Waldo's reply was telling: "No. You're still a joke. It's just not as funny anymore."

*

Philosopher David Hume said that any concept of personal identity had to be a fiction because it is made up of impressions that can fade or change, be added to or erased. For Hume, a stable personal identity is an illusion based on a series of impressions from which we make and project a self, a soul: "identity is nothing really belonging to these perceptions but is merely a quality, which we attribute to them, because of the union of their ideas in the imagination, when we reflect on them."[7] It is not just memory that is a construct. But ourselves.

Such a fluid conception of identity is at once frightening and thrilling. To be in constant change is to be unidentifiable, unrecognizable, even to ourselves. And it suggests not only that the person we were is no longer the person we are, but that there is no "person." No "there" there. So we are constantly attempting to build ourselves and others. We make legends, myths, and statues out of sand—and we try to build legacies as a brace against the tide. We build these identities, these images, these *characters*, then we protect them, forcing ourselves and others to inhabit the role. And I don't know what is more terrifying, the image in the mirror that keeps changing or the image we insist on. The one that says, I am, you are, we are—even as we change. We are so desperate for definition. To define ourselves and others. But a definition can only be made in retrospect. Which is to say that definition is death—a denial of change, of variation. And therefore, always a lie. When a staff member used to refer to my father as "a legend," he used to laugh it off. And I used to feel pride. But it's more complicated now that he is older. Even when he was young, the caricature, the cartoon of my father was out of proportion with the man. And now the two are incongruous to the point of inspiring cognitive dissonance. When the owners introduce a new staff member to him, they say, literally, "This is Joel Peckham, the myth, the legend" and my father responds with an odd mixture of satisfaction and resentment. His eyes brightening then hardening again, suspicious. Often, he just waves a hand and walks away, grumbling. Anxious to get away from it, to do something. The legend speaking only to who he was (or what he meant to others)—as if the person he is now has nothing left to offer. It must be terrifying to be replaced by a symbol. There is no speaking of the legend that does not seem absurd when in the presence of the actual man.

*

    Rachael and I have had a difficult and frightening spring. And I doubt my decision to return to camp every minute of the day. I'm distracted and unsettled, thinking about her, about us, constantly. And in the rare moments when I'm not, I feel waves of guilt. Then the evening comes and we fight. Most of the conversations start out positively. I look forward to hearing her voice and the first few minutes are cordial, loving. But then I'll lose reception and have to call her back, or she'll ask about my day and what I'm doing that night. And things escalate fast. She can't understand why I'm here, "why you left me. Do you know that for the first eight hours after you drove away, I still believed that you would turn around and come home. A part of me is still waiting. Where are you?" and I can't explain it to her because I can't really explain it to myself. I don't even know where to begin.

    As we talk, I'm standing in the middle of a dark access road that runs through the woods that border the soccer fields and outdoor hockey rink. When the phone buzzed, I had been on my way to a bonfire held in an unused parking lot at the edge of camp. I can see a faint orange glow through the trees, hear the warm murmur of drunken laughter. It's a moonless night, and looking up through the canopy of leaves I can see thousands of stars. My staff has talked me into going, overriding any objections (I'm tired. I'm too old for this crap). "C'mon, you've hardly left the band room or your cabin in two weeks," Eric said as we wrapped guitar cables, picking empty coffee cups from windowsills and amplifiers. "It'll be good for you. DT is going to bring a couple of guitars, and maybe the cajón. It'll be fun." "Just make sure he doesn't leave them there overnight," I tell him and he laughs. "All the more reason for you to show up. Consider it a professional obligation." My obsessive protectiveness of our equipment is an ongoing joke. Too often I have arrived at a practice to find a guitar missing from the band room and had to hunt the cabins searching for it. We've lost too many microphones, capos, tuners, and harmonicas to count, and campers continually steal aux cables so they can blast their music through the PA during socials. I take each theft, each unauthorized borrowing, each failure to return any item, no matter how small, as a personal affront and a sign of disrespect, and in these moments I become most like my father, who is famous for screaming at campers who dare to step on the infield dirt after he has raked it smooth and painted the lines, boiling over with righteous anger, completely incapable of understanding how people can be so lazy, so irresponsible, so disrespectful. It doesn't matter that our budget has grown to the point where almost anything in the room is replaceable ("Why do you get so upset? They'll just buy another one"). It's the principle of the thing. This is my equipment. My program. How dare you?

Motion sensor lights flicker on and off as groups of off-duty counselors walk silently past the laundry facility and the last three cabins that make up Sophomore Village, housing the youngest campers. It's 10:30 pm and you can still hear children laughing, stray flashlight beams raying out through screened windows.

There are easy answers to Rachael's questions, ones that make me look good, ones that center around my mother and my father and my need to be a good son—how, as soon as my mother told me that she and my father were returning, I felt that I had to go back as well. I simply couldn't imagine my father surviving a summer at Manitou without me there to help. Everything would fall on my mother—a prospect that frightened me. My father's confusion was growing worse, his rages more frequent. And too often, my mother was the target. The need to both help my father and support my mother are good reasons for me to be here.

But Rachael and I both know there's more to it than that. I'm a good son, but not that good. The problem is that a large part of me wants to be here. Needs to be here—for reasons that have nothing to do with my father's health. But even want and need feel like the wrong words. Compulsion feels closer to the mark. Addiction maybe. It would do no good at all to try to tell Rachael how many times I've almost thrown my belongings in the car and driven home (*then why don't you?*). How many times I had pulled off the highway on the long drive from West Virginia to Maine, thinking, what the hell am I doing?

"I guess I have to have cancer to be important enough," Rachael says, and I can't find a thing to say. It is true that had the biopsy come back with a different result, I would be home with her. "Thank God for Darius, at least." I want to tell her that she and Darius are the two most important people in my life. That I can't imagine living without them, but those words would only sound ironic under the circumstances. Here I am, after all, waking up every day without her. "I just don't understand. The Joel I know would be here right now."

It is a somewhat easy truth to say that we are made up of many selves. I have always believed this. That who we are in certain environments and circumstances and among certain people can completely change in different environments and situations or among different people. There may be an essential self, but it is always adapting, always under construction, trying on costumes to fit each performance. But what I am discovering is that these selves are not easily compartmentalized and are often irreconcilable. We do not simply leave one identity behind as we pick up a new one. No one fully disappears into the role. You take yourself, your *selves*, with you, wherever you go. And when they are at odds, warring with one another, that is a crisis. Who am I? JPJ, Jo Jo, Juniah, Joel, Doctor Peckham. Father, husband, widower, chronic pain sufferer, poet, musician, scholar, athlete, little boy singing take me out to the ballgame on a bench at the end of dinner, baseball glove eternally dangling from his left hand. I have never been comfortable with myself in the way that my father was or at least seemed to be when I was growing up. *He* was Joel Peckham. And that idea was mirrored back at him wherever he went. A strong and stable center beam for whatever circus tent people wanted to construct around him. And as I spoke to Rachael it was hard not to think that I had just run away from my life. To be another clown in the circus.

*

So we were barnstorming with the Varsity baseball team, riding that little orange school bus the Marcuses bought at auction. I think it might still be on the property somewhere, parked in the woods and left to rust out there. We should look for it sometime. It was a weird little thing with rattly seats that sat too high off the floor, so your feet didn't quite touch and it had windows that either came all the way down or didn't open at all. You had about 50/50 odds of getting where you were going—as long as the trip was under two hours there and back. And I swear you could smell gasoline and oil and exhaust fumes the whole time it was running. Thing was a death trap. So we were on the way to a game and you know how your dad is—all business. Kept shouting for us to sit the hell down and be quiet. But we were having a good time and a few of the kids were just jumping seat to seat. This one kid, I don't remember his name, he comes running down the aisle, and your dad doesn't even turn he just makes a fist and swings it up from the elbow like he's Chuck Norris, so the back of his hand hits the kid right in the forehead, knocking him flat. It got real quiet after that. Won the game. That kid had three hits, not counting the one he took from your pop.

*

The feeling of being "torn" is rare for me. My father brought me up with a simple ethos: figure out what the right thing to do is, then do it. "And don't expect to be thanked for it, either," I remember him telling me more than once. He still does. Back then he always seemed to have that clarity. He always seemed to know what was right and so he knew what to do. I remember driving back down 93 through southern Massachusetts from Winchester to Sharon. It had been maybe a few months since my grandfather has passed. We had taken my Nanna out to dinner, and he had refused to let her order a glass of wine. He refused even though he knew what that refusal would mean. The insults and recriminations. The hard looks from waiters and strangers at other tables. I remember trying to make myself sink into the padded bench of the booth, getting as low as possible, shying away from the harsh light of the faux Tiffany lamp hanging above the table in Nanna's favorite booth and favorite restaurant, The 99. *Just let her have the damned wine* I remember thinking, *please. What difference does it make?* Later, in the car, he would explain: "She shouldn't be drinking, Joel. And I know my brothers and sisters just give in. But when she climbs into a bottle she doesn't eat. Doctor says she weighs seventy-eight pounds. Seventy-eight pounds. Last week she passed out smoking in her bed. I found four burn holes in the mattress."

After the accident, I tried very hard to copy that decision-making process. And for a long time it was simple. Figure out what the best thing was for Darius first and me, second, and do that thing. Which is why coming back to camp was simple. Darius had lost a mother and a brother. He'd lost a home. I was suffering from chronic pain. I needed my parents to help me raise him. I needed a job. I needed a place where I could do physical therapy. I needed unconditional love. We both did.

*

In her email Rachael says that she has been trying to understand me, understand my decision to leave her in West Virginia. I start to read it before breakfast, sitting on the couch with a cup of bad coffee, steaming. It tastes like ashes in my mouth. Rachael has looked up my personality type using an "Enneagram"—a model based loosely on the teachings of Bolivian spiritual psychologist Oscar Ichazo. She has decided that I am a "Helper." I read through the identity type for "Helper" (which sounds good), someone driven by his need to love and be loved, who seeks to do good and is capable of "great self-sacrifice" and generosity when "healthy" but when "unhealthy" is "prideful, emotionally manipulative," and "needy" (which sounds bad). For some reason, it's the last word, "needy," that bothers me the most. Probably because I feel so damned needy right now. On the best of days I am not a morning person, but this morning is awful. I struggled to fall asleep then struggled to wake up. And when I did wake up, the light in the windowless bathroom went out and I accidentally tried to brush my teeth with a tube of Neosporin. And though I am not hungover, I've felt better.

I did end up going to the fire once Rachael and I had finally hung up and exchanged about twenty apology texts back and forth. When I walked up out of the shadows, I was immediately handed a bottle of bourbon by DT and embraced by my entire staff, who were clearly delighted to have me there. As were most of the younger staff. Directors don't generally show up at the staff fires. It is considered a compromising situation. My father used to tell me that "nothing good happens after 11pm." And this is generally good advice. A director doesn't want to be around if someone underage makes his way to a bonfire and gets drunk or belligerent. To encourage us to avoid those situations, some directors got together to build their own small firepit out along the road to the riflery range—a very neat, bench-lined circle with a carefully dug, symmetrical pit that would look appropriate in the backyard of any house on your average suburban cul-de-sac. By contrast, a staff fire looks and feels like a scene out of Delta House, complete with a bonfire made of wooden pallets and old broken furniture lit by gasoline. My face still feels a little raw and warm.

I'm not angry about Rachael's attempt at a personality diagnosis. In fact, the description seems fair. I felt ridiculous at the fire and stupid for drinking so much and staying out so late. I was even there for the inevitable sing-along to Oasis's "Wonderwall"—the stupidest song in the history of popular music—played enthusiastically by a British counselor with guitar skills that could generously be called adequate and a voice that could not. But I smiled in the flickering light and sang along about winding roads and blinding lights while wondering what on earth a "wonderwall" is and how a person could be one. I stared at the flames, dreading the lonely walk back to my empty bed. At least at the fire there was music and someone to talk to. But in the end, you can't avoid facing yourself in the mirror—even after the light has gone out.

I'm just tired. Tired of being generous, self-sacrificing, needy, and manipulative. Tired of trying to hang out with friends who are decades younger than I am. Tired of being me. I sit staring at the screen, scrolling through diagrams that looked torn from the pages of Harry Potter's spell book, thinking about which one would fit my father ("Challenger"), Darius ("Achiever"), Rachael ("Peacemaker").

The morning I left for the long drive to Maine we stood in the family room a few feet apart. The plan was that I would take Ivy with me. Her toys, bed, and bag of dog food were all piled by the door. My bags and guitars stacked and stuffed into our little Subaru. I had packed a few nights before as Rachael watched. "What if the results are bad," she said. "Then I won't go," I answered, "simple." And it was. We'd been in a state of anticipation for three weeks, losing sleep, and anxious. By the time Rach had gone through the surgical biopsy I think that hanging on to "the plan" had become a coping mechanism for both of us. Part of acting as if everything was going to be fine. As if we could simply press on with our lives, our plans. As if this were a blip. And normal was just around the corner. She would have the biopsy. It would come back negative. I would go to Maine. Everything was going to be fine. And I needed to believe that everything was going to be fine. This was nothing new, after all. Just a little more intense.

Rachael has fibrocystic breast tissue that requires constant monitoring. Most of the time the cysts, caused by fluid accumulation inside the glands of the breast, are uncomfortable but benign and will go away on their own. But they *can* become cancerous. We've had a few anxious doctors' appointments regarding cysts that seemed "suspicious" to the mammographer and required further testing. But this time they were more than suspicious, ranked from 1-6, one being clearly benign and six being almost certainly cancerous, with the cystic mass on the side of her left breast a 4 1/2. I had gotten Rachael's text while at a departmental meeting. Excusing myself, I walked out into the hallway, found the nearest bathroom, and dry-heaved in a stall.

We had arrived at the waiting room with little or no sense of what to expect. The biopsy had been harder than expected and Rachael's post-operative pain worse. She couldn't sleep and the scar was much larger than she had anticipated. "It's so ugly," she said. The breast surgery specialist, who I suspect was more than suspicious about the cyst, had decided in the operating room to completely remove the mass—in effect performing a lumpectomy. That choice alone had me thinking that the news might be very bad. And yet, I tried to reassure Rachael that there was nothing to worry about. I tried and failed to reassure myself of the same thing. But I hadn't slept in several days and felt as if I was moving though a nightmare. Rachael's grandmother had had the same condition, and for her it had resulted in a double mastectomy.

I had not expected the doctor to come out to the waiting room, to stand very close with his clipboard in hand. I found myself instinctively shrinking down into my seat, gripping Rachael's hand as if we were on a plane encountering bad turbulence. There was one other patient in the corner of the room: a middle-aged woman (or perhaps younger), filling out a medical form. I remember wondering if her perfectly coiffed blond hair, piled three inches above her head, was a wig. Christian rock music, the worst genre ever invented, played over the speakers. Dr. Jack Traylor stood above us, a thick-set, square-jawed man whose name sounded like something out of a Ken Follett novel. He had a silver crucifix pinned to one lapel, a rainbow pinned to the other. I felt small in his presence.

"Well, it's benign," he said. "Not even pre-cancerous."

Our elation at the news was intense but short-lived. Very quickly, I began to feel as if I were on a fast walk at an airport. That I was headed in one direction and had no agency to change it. I had told the owners that if the biopsy came back negative, I would make it to camp for the first day of orientation. I had told my staff this. I had told my mother this, who was desperate for both outcomes. "I can't imagine your dad being there without you," she said. "Are you sure Rachael won't come with you?" This feeling of being pulled along, of being acted upon instead acting is one I've found myself in the grips of many times in my life. I felt this way on the day of my first marriage. I felt this way the morning of the accident, when we all piled into a touring van that had no seatbelts. I felt it now. "Are you sure," Rachael asked. "Yes," I said, hugged her very lightly, trying hard not to put too much pressure on her sore chest and turned to walk out the door.

In the end, I left Ivy with her.

*

It interests me that though I have little recollection of the sound of Uncle Bobby's singing voice, almost everything else about that moment in the lodge seems cinematic in its clarity whenever "Puff the Magic Dragon" comes to mind or comes on the radio. Suddenly I remember the early evening light coming through the window. I remember the blue and white blankets on the bed. The walls were bluish gray, and we could see through some of the cracks between the planks where mosquitoes would slip through and torment us in our sleep. I remember Bobby in profile, the light of the window behind him, his hair floating up as if eternally charged by static. Behind him, a small grove of blackberry bushes—a massive glacial boulder sitting beside it. In *This is Your Brain on Music*, neuroscientist Daniel J. Levitin attempts to explain why music is so closely related to memory, why a song can not only bring us back to a moment but, even in patients who suffer from Alzheimer's or Parkinson's, a song can unlock a memory and seemingly—as is shown in documentaries like *Alive Inside*, suddenly, if temporarily, unlock or awaken a personality. We recover and uncover ourselves through music because the way we process it is relational and global. Music is not stored on one side of the brain, but bridges the lobes, stimulating multiple areas, even when listened to by non-musicians. As Levitin puts it, "your brain on music is the story of an exquisite orchestration of brain regions, involving both the oldest and the newest."[8] More importantly, "the music that you have listened to at various times in your life is cross coded with the events of those times. That is, the music is linked to events of the time, and those events are linked to the music."[9] So music not only brings us back to a moment in time, it stitches those moments and ourselves back together. "Your Brain on music . . . is all about connections."[10]

Maybe we *are* the connections we have made and the ones we have unmade. What we've held onto. What we've let go. What we have created along the way. The damage left behind when the jets fly off. And this is terrifying. And exhilarating and freeing. Because so much of that is beyond us. Out of our control. There is not a single note or melody or song that isn't rippling forward and back, entangled in every other song, waiting to be unleashed, released, unburied, unlocked, for us to hear it as if for the first time, for the first time. And sing along.

*

My first role in a Camp Manitou play was "The Baker's Wife" in an adaptation of Woody Allen's short sketch "Count Dracula." I don't possess much visual memory of that performance other than the green paint of the rec-hall floor and the tops of tennis shoes—those of actors and the audience spread in a semicircle below the stage. The part required me to stay hunched over a cane throughout the performance and that was fine with me, since I had a habit of forgetting my lines whenever I looked into the eyes of other actors, never mind a member of the audience—a product of a sometimes debilitating social anxiety that has followed me throughout my life. I wasn't just a shy child, I was actively frightened of people. So inward that I seemed out-of-it—"a total space cadet." In some ways, I still am. I also remember my highly affected impersonation of a Jewish grandmother, modeled after the cadences and inflections of Aunt Sis, the mother of then-owner Miles Marcus and wife of Henry—the man who first purchased the golf and fishing properties that were to become Manitou in 1947. I suspect that Marc Jacobs, our theater director, took a certain amount of glee in giving that role to me, the son of the "Baddest man on the mountain" and also one of two or three non-Jewish campers at Manitou. Marc and my father had an interesting relationship—one that stretched over twenty summers. They would occasionally butt heads when an infielder would be late for a practice or have to leave one early (or God forbid, miss one) for a rehearsal. But for all my father's grumbling, the two of them managed to accommodate each other pretty well. His reaction to hearing that I got the part was unbridled enthusiasm that was only dampened a little when he saw me in a dress and wig for the performance. Though I remember him wanting me to "get the hell out of that ridiculous getup" as soon as the play was over, I also remember him telling me how proud he was. He even presented me with a bag of gifts—a couple of Batman comic books, some crayons, and a sandwich bag full of dime-store candy. My father's support of my acting "career" was a surprise to some people at camp, but not to me. I think my silent inwardness worried and confused him. Both my mother and my father were extroverts, people who enjoyed being the focus of attention when all I wanted to do was disappear. He probably thought acting would pull me out of my shell. I'm not sure it works that way, not really.

What I loved about performing was disappearing into a character or a song. Amélie O. Rorty writes that "an actor dons masks, literally personae, that through which the sound comes, the many roles he acts."[11] I love that about acting. I loved the mask. In persona, I didn't have to worry about my words or how they would be construed. I didn't have to worry about the consequences of each action. I didn't have to be my father's son. I didn't have to not be my father's son. I could be Charlie Brown in *You're a Good Man, Charlie Brown*," Ike in *Sweet Betsy from Pike*, Joseph in *Joseph and his Amazing Technicolor Dreamcoat*, and Tony in *West Side Story*. At Manitou even the serious roles were often played for laughs—a product of having young boys slip on hose, wigs, and bras to perform as women in front of hundreds of whistling and catcalling fellow campers. But I treated every role with a stubborn absence of irony. A method actor before I knew what that meant, I played Charlie Brown like it was *Hamlet* and Joseph like *Henry V* (only not as funny). I didn't so much memorize lines as absorb them—often frustrating Marc when I would loosely improvise the dialogue. "You can't just make it up as you go along. This is a play. There are other actors. With cues." What I learned from acting was not how to be myself, but that I could be anyone. That identity was not a box I was trapped in, but a costume I could take on and off. And I learned to perform. And to feel the power and joy of performance. Of making a group of people feel what I felt. And applaud it. "Fake it 'til you make it," Marc would tell us. And I did that pretty well.

In memory, I often think of Marc and my father as mirrors of one another. Manitou's yin and yang. In literature we might use the term foil. But that isn't quite right. Marc didn't just contrast with my father—though there were certainly contrasts. My father was straight as an arrow, while Marc was unapologetically if not yet openly gay. My father was an athlete. Marc was an artist. My father was a Wasp. Marc was Jewish. My father was clean-shaven while Marc sported a bushy Tom Selleck moustache. My father strode through camp in coach's shorts and a Manitou staff shirt. Marc wore jeans and flannels pushed up at the elbows, stripping down to a t-shirt only when he was his most animated. But a mirror image is not its opposite. It is reflective. What my father and Marc shared was an almost irrational devotion to what they did—a single-minded focus and determination to not only do a thing but do it well—no shortcuts. When Marc would have 12-year-olds in the Rec Hall at midnight going over lines or when my father's practices stretched past recall and sometimes into evening activity, other directors would try to remind them "It's just camp," only to be hit by an almost identical outraged glare. The one that says "this is my field" "my stage" my territory and you would be wise to leave right now. They both turned a complete loss of perspective into a virtue by showing how much could be achieved when you took pride in what you did and fully, unreservedly, committed to it. And for that reason, they respected each other. I think my father also secretly loved and even envied Marc's iconoclasm. A jock throughout his life who wore a flat top all the way through college, my father had aspirations toward unconventionality.

Though in his case that meant driving a VW bus with a huge sunflower on the side of it while blasting Elvis and the Beatles though the radio. And to Marc it meant writing and performing an original musical devoted to the work of John Lennon, concluding it by simulating a heroin overdose on stage while the orchestral glissando to "A Day in A Life" roared in the background—all in front of hundreds of mostly prepubescent young boys.

My father will still tell you that that was his favorite Marc Jacobs production. I remember that he was in it, but not what he sang, and I must have been involved as well—part of the chorus at least. I was very young. But what I remember most is Marc up on stage, in the spotlight, rubber tourniquet tight around his arm, veins bulging, back arched, hips rising off the chair as the symphony rode the scale skyward—all the time he must have known that maybe twenty-five people in the audience knew what the hell was going on and most of those would have been horrified. It was beautiful and inappropriate. Uncomfortable and sensual. It was art.

Marc eventually left Manitou when he found out that the man he loved had contracted HIV, waiting until the final play was over before flying out to California to be with him and leaving his assistant Bob Doucette to finish off the summer.

He never came back.

*

    I have a lesson plan for one of the classes I teach at Marshall University, Introduction to Textual Analysis. It's fairly simple. I write on the board, "A character is" and ask each student to finish the sentence. By the end of class, the board is nearly white with chalk: A character is what a character does (and how and why s/he does it). A character is what a character says (and how and why s/he says it). A character is what a character thinks, believes, wants, fears, experiences, knows . . . . The list goes on, delving into territory about family, work, associations, culture, vocations and avocations, etc. etc. etc. Not once in twenty years of teaching has a student offered up, "a character is what a character remembers." And yet when I ask them directly what and who we are without our memories, I am confronted by long silences. Even with a chalkboard full of answers right in front of them.

*

"What's up, buddy?"

Corey has startled me, throwing his arms around my chest from behind and lifting me off the ground. Since the accident I've been easy to startle. Even when my students show up for scheduled appointments, if they walk through my office door while my back is turned and make the slightest sound, my body will react—muscles going rigid with adrenalin, hands flying up in a defensive posture. Sometimes I will literally jump off my chair. But I've learned to have a sense of humor about it. So I laugh as Corey sets me back down on the Rec Hall floor. The last staff meeting before Visiting Day has just ended, the counselors charging up from the bleachers to grab slices of pizza from boxes stacked on the stage. I had been keeping an eye on the equipment we had just begun to set up for the visiting day show. But I would have been here anyway. I generally show up for these meetings even though I don't really have to. Anything I have to say I can pass along to Corey to tell the staff. But there are very few music-related emergencies and I have long since stopped poking my nose into issues unrelated to my program. Still, I like watching Corey hold court. I like the rhythm of his speech and his odd, distinctive phrasing. "You pickin' up what I'm puttin' down?" "A.O. Good?" He manages that strange balance of intellect and blue-collar swagger in a way that reminds me of my father—a manner I have tried and failed to copy. I like watching him as he swivels back and forth on a drum throne he's borrowed for the purpose, making eye contact with each counselor as he runs through a series of notes –reminders of the director's expectations, what their individual responsibilities are, areas that need improvement and finally, presentation of "four-core-value" t-shirts, awards for staff members who have been having great summers. Every member of my staff except one, Ethan Gale, has achieved this distinction and tonight is his turn. I've been in Corey's ear about rewarding Ethan for a week now, bugging him about it at every meal. "You know, I love your staff, but I can't just give out awards to the music program every week."

"Well, they all deserve it. Besides, that way you know I'll show up."

"You just come for the free pizza."

I shouldn't have been surprised that Corey sought me out. I don't know if it is a product of his training, his observational skills, or some weird, ingrained ability to read and understand members of my family, but Corey has an almost spooky capacity for showing up when I am in my darkest moods or most difficult emotional places. He's the only person I know, other than the members of my staff and my family, who can correctly read my body language and facial expressions, what I say and what

I don't. I talk quite a bit but most of that talk is a kind of emotional cover-fire, a shitstorm of language meant to blind people to whatever I'm struggling with. Corey sees right through all of that.

"What's up, buddy?" is Corey's way checking in, of telling me that he's worried about me. The violent embrace a way of pulling me up and out of whatever cavern I have fallen into. He knows something is off. It's been a week since I've made the decision to leave camp early and I haven't told anyone but Rachael and Darius. I had tried to prepare my parents and staff early in the summer by telling them that I was considering leaving after our last show and heading home, and I've been telling most of the people I am close to that I won't be returning after this summer. But I think most people either didn't believe me or hoped I'd change my mind.

"You got a second?"

"Always."

*

    I would not say that the approach of Visiting Day brings out the best in me. I tell myself that I will stay calm, that we've done this year after year and it always goes well. Even in the years that it doesn't, when we just don't have the musicians or the singers, the parents love the show. We've had kids on stage with guitars that aren't plugged in, kids singing into dead microphones, and playing keyboards with no instrument cable attached to it whatsoever (all deliberate decisions) and the parents cheer and applaud like they are attending a Springsteen concert. And the truth is, the performances are usually good. Kids learn fast and, with exceptions, are less prone to stage fright than most adults. What they do in the band room is pretty close to what they perform on stage. This year's lineup of songs, a mix of crowd-pleasing classics and Top 40 hits, has come together remarkably well. We have the vocalists and that's 90 percent of the battle. More importantly, each one of my vocalists is a skilled performer and frontman who knows how to work the stage and the crowd in front of it. And my staff has worked these kids hard. We also have a great set-up, having reclaimed the old stage by replacing one wall of the band room with sliding, garage-style doors that can easily be rolled back to open up into the main hall. It feels wonderfully appropriate that our final performance of the summer, my final performance at Manitou, will be on the same stage where I had played the baker's wife forty years before. And the set looks beautiful. We don't have to move any equipment, just push the drums to the middle of the room, face the amps and PA outward, and boom, it's showtime: the practice room exposed in all its maroon and gold psychedelic glory, transformed into a stage. Still, I'm on edge, running wires, positioning and repositioning amps, performing a sound check. Eric is doing most of the technical work, plugging and unplugging cables into the mixing board as I strum a chord on a guitar or count into a microphone.

    I've already snapped at Eric once. A 20-year-old counselor named Griffen asked him to put a banner up above the stage. Griffen is a "Dean," captain of one of the four "College League" teams—an honor given mostly to former campers who showed leadership skills. And Griffen was well-deserving of that honor. He's a great kid. But he is also unlucky because today he's sharing his meeting place with us, with me. On Visiting Day the owners like to have the parents visit College League meeting places to give them a feel for what this intracamp competition is about—to hear the cheers and get a sense of the camaraderie competition can instill. In preparation, Griffen wanted to raise a banner and add a little color, a little "hype," to his meeting. Totally reasonable. But my stress level was already pushing into the red, and I wasn't in the mood to be accommodating.

"We're trying to work here. That can wait until we're done" I snapped, dismissing him, thinking that would be the end of it.

But Eric is a people pleaser and so when I had stepped out to talk to Rachael on my cell phone, he had grabbed a ladder from somewhere and tried to quickly put the banner up before I got back. Seeing him up there on the top rung, on a stage, twenty feet off the ground, precariously reaching upward with one hand, a hammer dangling from the other, two nails in his mouth, triggered a moment of fear, leading to anxiety, and then directly to irrational rage. "Eric! Get the hell down from that ladder right now," I shouted, turning toward a suddenly very concerned young man who was now backing up with his hands half raised like he was warding off a bear— "It's not his fault. I asked him to do it."

"I know it's not his fault. It's *your* fault, Griffin. He works for me. Not you."

"I was just . . ."

"Leaving!"

Like every time I've lost my temper, I know I will regret it. But in this moment the adrenaline rush runs like a current through me, a cathartic release of tension, anxiety, and stress that is like a darker version of what it feels like to play music. And seeing someone become afraid of you, their eyes widening, their body language turning toward defense, is powerful. In these moments, adrenaline sparking and spidering through my chest and back, I understand why my father indulges this part of himself so frequently. Right now, I am in control of my world. Or I think I am. As soon as the moment is over, the large screen doors of the Rec Hall rattling shut as the young man hustles down the hill, my reptile brain withdrawing back into the shadows, I feel remorse, exhaustion. Reuben used to call what comes next the "Joel Peckham Junior apology tour"—in which I track down the person I yelled at and ask forgiveness repeatedly over several days, then track down anyone who might have been present for my tantrum, apologizing to them too, then spend the rest of the summer trying to forgive myself—long after everyone on staff has decided that this is all hilarious and has turned it into a story they will laughingly retell over drinks in my cabin, complete with comically exaggerated facial expressions and hand gestures. "You should have seen his face!"

All part of the JPJ experience.

Eric is already trying to stifle the giggles. "Eric . . . ."

"I know, boss. You're sorry. Got it."

"I'm going for a walk." I need one. I'm a basket case. I make a mental note to track Griffin down at dinner. He's a good kid. He deserved better. I try to take a series of deep, cleansing breaths as I walk up the hill and out into left field. Everything feels like it's coming at me and slipping away too fast. Four weeks at Manitou has this way of seeming like four years and four minutes all at once and as my time here has shrunk from weeks to days I have become intensely emotional. Always on the edge of tears and laughter. The day before I had been walking back from a coffee break at the dining hall to find all of my campers and staff outside the band room on the grass. Hudson was openly sobbing. Alex had his hands in his hair like he wanted to pull it out in chunks. And little Max looked stunned, sitting on a large rock and staring off at nothing. Jake was, well, Jake was over by himself on the basketball court, torturing a caterpillar with a stick. I could feel something drop in my gut "Shit," I thought, "they know."

Andy hurried past the group to reach me before they closed around me in a tight circle, saying "I didn't know you hadn't told them yet. I swear. I just said they needed to make this good because it would be your last Visiting Day." I just stared at him in disbelief. "Do they know *when* I'm leaving?" I had only just told Jon Deren that I would be leaving as soon as our last show was over, a full band performance at Oakfest, a yearly outdoor music and food festival hosted by the town of Oakland, only a week away and two weeks before the end of the summer. He understood. I don't think he liked it. But he understood, agreeing with me that the program was in great shape and that almost any member of my staff was trained and ready to lead it.

"Jesus, Andy, we have a show to prepare for. I don't have time for this." The truth is, I'd been afraid to tell them—not because I thought they would be hurt or tearful. I knew they would be sad but also that these kids love me the way kids love—intense adoration and affection followed by amnesia. Moving on from disappointment as quickly as puppies distracted by a new toy. I know better than anyone else how easily even the most beloved camp characters are replaced, becoming part of the folklore of the place or simply being forgotten—sometimes while they are still around. And I'm fine with that. A child's mourning period should be as brief as a squall blowing in over the lake. Learning to deal with change is part of growing up. But to tell them, to say it out loud, risked making it real somehow. I knew that once I had spoken the words, there was no going back. And I wonder if Andy, on some level, hadn't known that, hadn't hoped that forcing me to confront these boys would make me think about what I was doing. To make me face how big this was for me, for him. And the truth was that I didn't know what it would mean for me. Who would I be without this place, these people. Without the kids and the staff. Without my father out on the ball fields hitting fungoes high into a hazy blue summer sky.

I thought of Corey, sitting with me on the bleachers, in the dark. "It sounds to me like you know what you're gonna do, what you have to do. I know you're worried about your dad. But he'll be ok. So will your mom. They're on my radar. And look, we all want you here. But you have to want to be here or it's not good for anybody. Not good for the kids or your staff or you. So go. Go be with your wife and kid. You don't owe this place anything you haven't already given it. You don't need anyone's permission. Who knows, maybe someday things will change. Maybe not. If they do and you need this place, it'll still be here. You gotta tell the kids, though."

I looked at them thinking, "It's time. Time to stop performing. Time to step away. I have a home, and this isn't it. I have a family and it isn't here." So I walked with Andy back into the circle of wide-eyed children and tried to put a period to the end of the sentence.

*

  I remember I was having a really bad summer. Maybe it was '81 or '82. Sometimes when you're struggling this is a great place to be, you know? Yeah. But it's also strange. It's not like your problems disappear when you come through the gates—they just kind of seem a long way off. And since you can't really do anything about them while you're here, you go with it. Like it's Neverland or something. But the world keeps going. And sometimes you can't shut it out. And sometimes being so far away just makes the problems feel worse, bigger somehow. Well, it was just one of those summers already. Girlfriend broke up with me over the phone. I was having some problems at the school where I work and my job was feeling a little shaky. Then about three weeks in I get called to the office. It's my mom. And she's just crying so hard I couldn't make out what she was saying. My dad had a heart attack. A big one. Widowmaker. He was never even sick. He was alive and then, he wasn't. Here then gone. And my dad and I weren't in a very good place, just then. So I hung up the phone and walked across the flagpole area, stunned, crossed the basketball court and just sat on the bleachers crying. Head in my hands. I don't know how long I was there. And then I feel this hand on my back, rubbing it in small circles between the shoulder blades. I guess he overheard me on the phone from his office. I mean he followed me and then just sat there rubbing my back. I don't know how long. Your dad's a great talker but he didn't talk. We just sat there and he let me cry and he waited and waited until I was ready to speak. This was the middle of camp, free-play, kids playing basketball, announcements over the P.A. And he sat there with me for like two hours, straight through evening activity, letting me talk. I'll never forget that. Never.

Visiting Day, Music Program, 2018

Blame it on Me—George Ezra
Martin Long—Guitar and Lead Vocals; Eric Jonson—Keyboards; Ethan Gale—Guitar; Julia Grimmet—Drums and Vocals; Dave Thirimur—Bass

Pompei—Bastille
Eric Jonson—Lead Vocals and Keyboards; Stephanie Fernandes—Vocals; Joel Peckham—Vocals and Guitar; Ethan Gale—Guitar; Julia Grimmet—Drums; Dave Thirimur—Bass

You and I Both—Jason Mraz
Andre Esau—Lead Vocals; Jagger Zemachson—Lead Guitar; Eli Weingarten—Rhythm Guitar; Jack Bradner Rhythm Guitar; Griffin Krupp—Bass; Oliver Aizer—Bass; Reid Rosenberg—Drums; Adam Balbale—Keyboard and Vocals

Beat It—Michael Jackson
Adam Balbale—Lead Vocal; Rider Rush—Lead Vocal; Logan Waks—Lead Guitar; Eli Weingarten—Rhythm Guitar; Jack Bradner—Rhythm Guitar; Griffin Krupp—Bass; Oliver Aizer—Bass; Reid Rosenberg—Drums; Andre Esau—Percussion; Ferdinand Castera—Keyboards

Fix You—Coldplay
Stephanie Fernandes—Lead Vocals; Eric Jonson—Vocals and Keyboards; Joel Peckham—Vocals; Ethan Gale—Guitar; Andy Ambat—Lead Guitar; Julia Grimmett—Drums; Dave Thirimur—Bass

Suspicious Minds—Mark James/Elvis Presley
Alex Brooks and Hudson Brown—Lead Vocals; Maxwell Apple—Vocals; Alex Wood—Vocals; Jake Wadley—Lead Guitar; Henry Gretsch—Rhythm Guitar; Nate Meyers—Bass; Noah Katzman—Drums

Superman—Goldfinger
Hudson Brown—Lead Vocals; Alex Brooks—Vocals; Maxwell Apple—Vocals; Nate Meyers—Bass; Jake Wadley—Lead Guitar; Henry Gretsch—Keyboards; Carter Braxton—Drums

Radioactive—Imagine Dragons

Maxwell Apple—Lead Vocals; Alex Brooks—Vocals; Hudson Brown—Rhythm Guitar and Vocals; Nate Meyers—Bass; Jake Wadley—Lead Guitar; Ferdinand Castera—Keyboards; Noah Katzman—Drums

Africa—Toto
Stephanie Fernandes—Lead Vocals; Eric Jonson—Vocals and Keyboards; Joel Peckham—Vocals and Guitar; Ethan Gale—Guitar; Andy Ambat—Lead Guitar; Julia Grimmett—Drums; Dave Thirimur—Bass

Hallelujah—Leonard Cohen
Hudson Brown—Lead Vocals; Stephanie Fernandes—Vocals; Eric Jonson—Keyboards

Tighten Up—The Black Keyes
Eric Jonson—Keyboards; Ethan Gale—Lead Guitar and Vocals; Julia Grimmett—Drums; Dave Thirimur—Bass

Don't Look Back in Anger—Noel Gallagher
Eric Jonson—Vocals and Keyboards; Joel Peckham—Vocals and Guitar Ethan Gale—Lead Guitar

*

 There is a video of the last song we played that day, a cover of "Don't Look back in Anger," one of Eric's favorites. I am no fan of Oasis, whom I have always considered more of a Beatlesque pastiche than an actual band. In fact, for a long time, I had a program-wide Oasis ban (that also included Billy Joel, Phil Collins, and the Eagles). But this song is sturdy and familiar in a way that reaches beyond nostalgia by fully leaning into it so that the lyrics and music double back on each other, every part of the song performing what it's trying say. I'm suspicious that the Gallagher brothers stumbled into this rather than planned on it. As my father would say after watching a right fielder stumble into a diving catch, "even a blind squirrel can find a nut once in a while."

 Nothing in their catalogue is nearly this good—a song about the past, about memory and regret that sounds as if it were written by using pieces of other songs, half-remembered, picked apart and put back together.

 Eric and I have simplified the instrumentation, stripping the arrangement of pretension—no drums, no orchestration. I'm playing Big Blue, a royal blue Washburn dreadnought I found on discount because no one would buy it in that color. I liked it immediately. The way it stood out from everything else in Down Home Music—its almost mandolin-like brightness reminding me of my first guitar, a Seagull Susie bought me for my birthday when I turned 30. I have turned the treble all the way up. Ethan sits on a Cajon because he couldn't find a strap for my casino. This has the unintended but not unpleasant effect of causing a sympathetic vibrational rattle, fading into a buzz similar to a snare. Throughout, he plays subtle licks and a solo I had worked out for him—a simple progression of notes based on an A minor pentatonic scale, the first scale I teach on guitar. One I probably taught him years ago when he couldn't have been more than nine years old. Anyone could play it, but he plays it well, tastefully, with soul. Eric is on keys, just playing the chords, occasionally arpeggiating. We've slowed down the tempo and given the rhythm a bit more swing, so it is almost a blues. We want the song to breathe. To ache a little.

 The point is not the musicianship anyway. No one is showing off. We want everything to be about the voices, the harmonies we have layered, structuring the song to emphasize the interplay Eric and I can achieve when we are locked in, not competing but complementing each other's tone. We switch back and forth between melody and harmony. Both of us confident the other can hit the notes. My hair is long from a summer away from any barber. I'm wearing a navy-blue staff shirt—an accommodation to conformity that everyone who has seen me today has made a point to comment on. We look tired but relaxed. Comfortable with each other.

What you can't see in the frame is that we are playing to an almost empty house. The main show with the kids has been over for a while now. There were the usual glitches, the drummer forgetting to come back in after a planned break during Michael Jackson's "Beat It," a guitar solo that got lost in the mix because Jake accidentally turned his amp down when he intended to turn it up. But overall, the show was a hit. We had planned to have the staff band alternate with campers, but the kids were playing and singing so well and the parents were enjoying it so much, that we just handed the show over to them, letting them build momentum as they went. I found myself crying at several points. The kids just seemed so brave. So happy. Throwing themselves at the songs with real joy. We'd pushed two sets of bleachers right up against the stage, so their parents would be almost on top of them as they played. And it felt intimate and charged. After fifteen minutes we basically had a full house with people walking in from all over the camp to listen to the music. And for forty-five minutes their children put on the best show we've ever done. Once the last note was played on Leonard Cohen's "Hallelujah," the happy parents left with our blessing. We were exhausted by then anyway. Tired of smiling and shaking hands. Tired of acting the parts of responsible music educators. And grateful to just play music and enjoy ourselves. The result is that the counselor set is more like a practice if not a jam—part of a conversation we have been having all summer, one I've been having for years. Some of our friends who are unassigned to an activity area (and a few who have used this relatively unstructured time to sneak off) have filtered in to listen. But we are playing for and to each other now. One last time.

The last several hours of the day are left open for parents to shoot baskets, go for a swim, use the batting cages, or take their children out of camp for fast food meals and supply trips to Walmart. Even the video guy is gone, having slipped off to see if there are any lobster rolls left from the catered lunch. He has left the camera on "record" with the promise that we would turn it off when we were done and bring it back to the video room when we broke down the set. We also know that there is an audience out there that we can't see and for whom we are a soundtrack to this summer day, conscious that from our position at the center of camp, at the top of the hill, the music will carry all the way down to the waterfront and out over the fields. A few counselors have taken up space in the bleachers we had pulled in for the show. My father usually mans the batting cages during this late period and, most years, will listen from outside the building as he feeds yellow composite balls into the jugs machine, quietly laughing to himself as he watches middle-aged men in sandals swat and flail, trying to impress their wives and sons with their athletic prowess (you can actually hear the occasional ping of a bat hitting a ball on a few of the videos). But this year, he's shut it down early and sits right up front, next to my mother, eyes bright and focused. His hat pulled low like a cowboy's.

In *Musicophilia* Oliver Sacks devotes a chapter to the effects of music on the severely demented, drawing both from what he knows of neurology and from anecdotal experience with music therapy. He concludes that "Music is part of being human, and there is no human culture in which it is not highly developed and esteemed. Its very ubiquity may cause it to be trivialized in daily life: we switch it off, hum a tune, tap our feet, find the words of an old song going through our minds, and think nothing of it. But to those who are lost in dementia, the situation is different. Music is no luxury to them, but a necessity, and can have a power beyond anything else to restore themselves to themselves, and to others, at least for a while."[12] I believe this to be true for all of us, regardless of the condition of our memories. When I am playing music with other people, when I am singing with other people, I am most who I am. I rediscover myself and come back to myself. I am fully a body and bodiless. Middle aged and young. The chords find themselves and I forget my hands, allowing them to do what they do. My voice slips into place beside Eric's, and even though I am singing someone else's song this does not feel like a performance or a copy of something else. I feel I am breaking through all that to something that connects all the dots of who I am, have been and will be, gliding forward and backward and sideways through time like the water bugs I'd watch from the fishing rock as a child, skittering and gliding across reflections of clouds forming and dissipating, soaring in a rippling sky above the flickering sunfish, the undulating pike. Dots that include not only the people on the stage with me but every stage I've stood on and every person I've played with or to—Chase is there—an echo of my voice. Reuben sits on the empty drum throne, Davis adds a lick, John comes in on bass, Andy Arenson leans in, listening—the sound swelling around us all.

And my father's presence fills the room. But not only his presence, my mother too, eternally young with one foot hooked in a ski-rope, her arms holding a ski aloft above her. My grandfather in his nursing home bed, begging us to take him out for ice-cream as Sinatra played on the radio, Cyrus as I sang him to sleep above his crib, Susie in her ripped jeans, carving a rose onto a canvas to Muddy Waters, eternally "ready, ready's anybody can be." Rachael in white snowpants and pink parka, sledding with my son down a hill in New Hampshire, in Ohio, in West Virginia. Rachael, the night before her biopsy, in my arms, unable to sleep, asking me to sing to her. And all the other voices, all the other songs. Those I have listened to, and who have listened to me, their heartbeats and rhythms both distinct and complementary, become part of a polyrhythmic yet unified whole.

I don't know what my father is thinking but I know that he is here completely and also far away and deep within himself, his body relaxed, and calm. His lips moving silently, repeating the chorus of a song he doesn't know and does in the way that all songs contain so many songs and singers, how through repetition and pattern they create anticipation, of the next beat, the next word, the next note. Our knowledge based on a shared library of melodies we know beyond our knowing. Where is he? Who is he in this moment? 19 and jitterbugging to Bill Haley and his Comets in the high school gymnasium? Singing along at the top of his lungs to Eddie Rabbit's "I Love a Rainy Night" as he steers our Chevy van down Route 95 past the South of the Border sign toward Florida, his children asleep on a mattress he has lain across the back seat, a light rain stippling the windshield, as the wipers seem to keep the beat? And I know who he is. He is my father.

And right now that simple truth is all that matters.

And I know this is fleeting and will pass like every moment does and that this is its beauty. I can feel the summer slipping away with each note. And I want to stay here as long as possible because I know what lies on the other side, whatever it is, wherever I am will only include this song as memory and that this too will fade as I do, will change as I do. We move into harmony before splitting apart, each of us asking the listener to move away from anger and toward acceptance even for a moment. Eric looking straight at me while I sing directly to my father.

And whatever wolves this song, this moment, this place, has held at the door—my doubts and insecurities, my loves and resentments, and all my angers, will come pouring through. A reckoning. Because music is made of not only melody, tempo, and rhythm, but time, duration. You can ruin a thing by refusing to let it go, hammering the chorus again and again until you are sick of it, or dragging out the solo in an act of unseemly self-preservation, until it unmakes the song. Everything beautiful has to end if only so it may linger in the silence that follows, so it can come back again and again with all of its associative force and possibility.

I don't remember everything or anything I was thinking or feeling in that moment. I can hardly remember what it was to be that person now. I'm surprised and delighted to meet him again. And I am surprised to hear myself flub the final note. Just a little, a loss of control, a quavering too high on the word "today" so I'm forced to recover, sliding the final syllable back into place in a casual trill. And it somehow sounds exactly right. A happy accident. Authentic.

We stop, beaming at each other. Eric nods. Ethan erupts into a happy smile. There is a beat of silence. And then my father's rough and quiet voice, just before the recording stops: "That was beautiful. Just beautiful."

Acknowledgements

Grateful acknowledgement is given to Henry Stanton and Uncollected Press for believing in this work and to Rachael Peckham and Darius Atefat-Peckham for being my first readers and for always supporting me with love and compassion. Thanks as well to Michele Schiavone for her work editing this manuscript, to Lily Jurskis for her beautiful cover art, and to Austin O'Connor for somehow making me look good in the author's photo. Thanks to my family, especially my mother Jeanne and my sisters, Tina and Lisa. I also wanted to thank Camp Manitou owners present and past, especially David Schiff, John Deren, Bob Marcus, Amy Marcus, Miles Marcus, and Sue Marcus. Their generosity toward my family can never be repaid. Thanks to Marc Jacobs, forever my theater director, and all members of my music staff, especially Davis McGraw, John Salvage, Tristan Hewitt, Andy Ambat, Dave Thirimur, Reuben Ambat, Julia Grimmett, Stephanie Fernandes, Eric Jonson, John Fernandes, Chase Adkins, Ethan Gale, Zach Burns, Miles Sheft, Jared Allen, David Slitsky, and Reid Moak. Thanks to all generations of Manitou baseball staff, especially Phil Silverman, Herbie Magid, Kevin Stonesifer, David Bernstein, and Michael Poretsky for loving my father almost as much as I did.

Finally, thanks to Nayt Rundquist and New Rivers Press for publishing an early version of chapter 14 in their anthology, *Unbound: Composing Home* under the title, "Ghosts of Summer."

Joel Peckham has published nine collections of poetry and nonfiction, most recently Bone Music (SFAU), MUCH (UnCollected Press), Body Memory (New Rivers), and the spoken word LP, Still Running: Words and Music by Joel Peckham (EAT poems). His new and selected poems, *Any Moonwalker Can Tell You* is forthcoming from SFA Press in the early summer of 2024. With Robert Vivian, he also co-edited the anthology, *Wild Gods: The Ecstatic in Contemporary Poetry and Prose*. He is an Associate Professor of American Literature and Creative Writing at Marshall University.

"If a book can be a song, the pages of *Gone the Sun* sing. They sing remembering and forgetting. Grief and Endurance. Present and past. In the present time of the is memoir-in-fragments, Joel Peckham spends a last summer as music director at Manitou, the boys camp that has been part of his life since he was a child. Manitou summons Peckham's past—his father, his lost wife, his lost son. But there are songs of redemption those weeks too. This is a book that sings both back and forward with love, urging us all home."

Karen Salyer McElmurray, author of *Voice Lessons* and *I Could Name God in Twelve Ways*

"In *Gone the Sun*, Peckham writes about his loving, sometimes fraught history with Manitou, a summer camp he and his father worked at for many years. As his father declines into dementia the middle-aged Peckham—still working summers at the camp between semesters as a college professor—muses upon time, upon loss, and the various selves we inhabit as we age. This is a beautiful, heartbreaking book, but heartbreaking in the most resonant, emotionally intelligent, and illuminating way possible."

Sue William Silverman, author, *Acetylene Torch Songs: Writing True Stories to Ignite the Soul*

Notes:

---

[1] Oliver Sacks, *Musicophilia: Tales of Music and the Brain,* New York: Vintage Books, 2007, 372.
[2] See John Locke, *Essay Concerning Human Understanding*, 2nd ed., ch. 27, (1964), reprinted in John Perry, ed., *Personal Identity*, Berkeley: U California Press., 1975, 39-40.
[3] Steven Pinker, *How the Mind Works,* New York: Norton, 1997, 534.
[4] David Huron, "Is Music an Evolutionary Adaptation?" in *The Cognitive Neuroscience of Music,* edited by I Peretz and R. Zatorre, Oxford: Oxford UP., 2003, 57-75.
[5] Galen Strawson, "Against Narrativity," *Ratio,* 2004, Vol. 17, No. 4, 428-452.
[6] Amélie Oksenberg Rorty, "A Literary Postscript: Characters, Persons, Selves, Individuals" in *The Identities of Persons*, edited by Amélie Oksenberg Rorty, Berkely: U California P, 1976, 306.
[7] David Hume, *A Treatise of Human Nature*. Ed. L. A. Selby-Bigge. Oxford: Clarendon Press, 1975, 185.
[8] Daniel J. Levitin, *This is Your Brain on Music: The Science of a Human Obsession,* New York: Dutton, 2006, 125.
[9] Levitin, 162.
[10] Levitin, 188.
[11] Rorty, 309.
[12] Sacks, 385.

www.ingramcontent.com/pod-product-compliance
Lightning Source LLC
Chambersburg PA
CBHW020256090426
42735CB00009B/1106